JOŽE PLEČNIK

JOŽE PLEČNIK

Architect: 1872–1957

**Edited by François Burkhardt,
Claude Eveno, and Boris Podrecca**

Translated by Carol Volk

The MIT Press
Cambridge, Massachusetts
London, England

Original French edition © Editions du Centre Pompidou/CCI, Paris, 1986
No. d'editeur: 499
ISBN: 2-85850-330-3
Dépôt légal: March 1986

Translation into French of the German texts: Guy Ballangé, Jeanne Ettoré
Translation of Slovenian texts: Andrée Lück-Gaye
Translation of Czechoslovak texts: Erika Abrams

Conception of the original French catalog *Jože Plečnik, Architecte, 1872–1957*, by François Burkhardt, Claude Eveno, Boris Podrecca, CCI Editions. Published in conjunction with the exhibition *Jože Plečnik, Architecte*, produced by Le Centre de Création Industrielle and presented between March and May of 1986 in the CCI Gallery of the Centre National d'Art et Culture Georges Pompidou.

This book was set by Graphic Composition in a digitized version of Perpetua, a typeface originally designed in the 1920s by Eric Gill. The book was printed and bound by Halliday Lithograph in the United States of America.

Book design: Claudia Thompson

Library of Congress Cataloging-in-Publication Data

Jože Plečnik, architecte; 1872–1957. English.
  Jože Plečnik, architect, 1872–1957 / edited by François Burkhardt, Claude Eveno, and Boris Podrecca ; translated by Carol Volk.
    p.   cm.
  Translation of: Jože Plečnik, architecte, 1872–1957.
  Bibliography: p.
  Includes index.
  ISBN 0-262-02290-7 (hard back)
  1. Plečnik, Jože, 1872–1957—Exhibitions.   2. Architecture, Modern—20th century—Yugoslavia—Exhibitions.   3. Plečnik, Jože, 1872–1957—Criticism and interpretation.   I. Burkhardt, François, 1936– .   II. Eveno, Claude.   III. Podrecca, Boris, 1940– .   IV. Title.
  NA1453.P55A4   1989
  720'.92'4—dc19   89-2815
                                                        CIP

Contents

Preface

François Burkhardt

In presenting the work of Jože Plečnik, Le Centre de Création Industrielle pays tribute to an architect who left his mark on twentieth-century architecture but who has been unjustly overlooked, because of the evolution of criticism and the modern movement.

The current questioning of fundamental assumptions of the modern era allows us to appreciate this architect's output, with his rigorous ethics yet very eclectic sense of form: modernist in some ways, classical in others, but always firmly rooted in his birthplace—Slovenia. A solitary pioneer, he pursued ideas that often challenged the wisdom of contemporary trends. In his book *Complexity and Contradiction in Architecture,* Robert Venturi pointed out that his works are interesting precisely because of these contradictions.

The idea for an exhibition devoted to Plečnik initially came from a small group interested in, even passionate about, his work: art historian and scholar Damjan Prelovšek, author of a book on the architect's Viennese period, and Boris Podrecca, the architect responsible for organizing the very first exhibition in 1967 as well as several seminars on Plečnik's work at various universities, who was entrusted with the installation of his work at the gallery of the Centre de Création Industrielle in the Centre National d'Art et Culture Georges Pompidou. My association with this initiative, in addition to my duties at the Centre Pompidou, stems from my interest in cultural revivals. Lojze Gostiša, who arranged for the first Plečnik exhibition in Yugoslavia, placed his outstanding collection of photographic archives at our disposal, and co-ordinated the part of the exhibition that was prepared in Ljubljana. Together, these collective efforts and expertise have made possible the first Jože Plečnik retrospective; after Paris, the exhibition will travel throughout Europe.

This book is composed of historical texts that place Plečnik and his work in cultural and historical context, in Vienna, Prague, and Ljubljana. The second part presents a typological and morphological analysis of Plečnik's architecture.

Neither the exhibition nor the catalog would have been possible without the helpful support of the Ljubljana Museum of Architecture and of its director, Petr Krečič, attentive guardian of the Plečnik archives.

We would also like to express our gratitude to the many lenders to the exhibition, to all those who made this project possible, and to the authorities of the Socialist Republic of Slovenia and of the city of Ljubljana, who saw in this initiative a means of bringing attention to Slovenian culture and paying homage to one of their prestigious sons. Without the moral and material support of these people, the exhibition could not have possessed the breadth that it does.

Finally, our hope is that this exhibition and catalog will revitalize the debate, dormant these past fifteen years, over the relationship between form and content in architecture. We would like to show that an architecture that expresses the collective interest is "committed" and that form is a symbolic expression that allows for communication with society.

Such discussion seems indispensable if architecture is to bring back the vital dimension it has lost: its social role. Jože Plečnik's work provides a brilliant example for this debate.

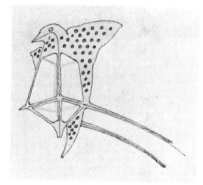

BACKGROUND

A Slavic Gaudi?

A Few Remarks about Jože Plečnik

Friedrich Achleitner

Jože Plečnik's artistic evolution was shaped by the intersection of the three cultures in which he lived. Slovenia is situated within the limits of the Roman and Byzantine worlds, at the Romano-Slavic linguistic border. In the nineteenth century, the upper classes of these regions were all of German culture, whose center was Vienna. Plečnik was therefore condemned to multilingualism from the start, with the added complexity of having a minority language as his mother tongue. He was forced to conduct his education and professional career in a foreign language, that is to say, in a foreign culture. Jože Plečnik remained deeply attached to his Slovenian homeland throughout his life, an attachment reinforced by strong family ties. This devotion, and the accompanying emotional force, was not only to be a source of conflict during his years of apprenticeship, but was also to mark his professional life.

Plečnik's multicultural identity provides the backdrop for the conflict that was to break out between this son of peasants and craftsmen (his father was a cabinetmaker) and the upper-middle-class German Nationalists, as well as the conflict between the strictly obedient Catholic—even naive with respect to the big city—and the liberal, utilitarian bourgeoisie of Viennese high society, best represented by his professor, Otto Wagner. Jože Plečnik was not content merely to have contacts with Pan-Slavist ideology; he also maintained ties with the nationalism of the Crown States, which daily became more vital and aggressive. Although all forms of national romanticism, even German, were deeply foreign to Otto Wagner, his school must have been a battleground for national temperaments (German, Jewish, Czech, Moravian, Slovak, Hungarian, Slovenian, and Italian) or at the very least a forum for discussing different national architectures.

The young Plečnik must have viewed the "imperial city," the sumptuous vitality of Viennese architecture at the time of the Ringstrasse's completion, as a provocation, even as a threat. Only this can explain the passion he displayed for his work, his passage from unbounded pride to despair, but also his constant skepticism and criticism of urban civilization.

Whereas most of Wagner's students followed their master's doctrine more or less without question, Plečnik began to distance himself surprisingly early. It is possible that his friendship with the Czechs, in particular with Jan Kotěra, was instrumental in this.

Like Pavel Janák, Plečnik never formulated his critique in theoretical writings; he stated his opinions in occasional declarations, and evidence of them can be seen in his work. He shared neither Otto Wagner's belief in progress and positive rationalism, nor the unconditional abandon to the spirit of the times advocated by most of the Secessionists. As paradoxical as it may seem, he took modernity too seriously to accept its falling victim to its own superficiality. He possessed neither the cynicism nor the sense of cultural superiority of the big-city dweller; his visual multilingualism placed much finer instruments of differentiation in his hands. He scorned both "hack writers" and theoreticians, but this did not prevent him from devoting all his thought to theoretical problems.

Plečnik embraced Western humanist civilization, traces of which still color historicism, with a certain naiveté. This alone explains his shock upon discovering the original sources in Italy. This also explains why, having seen them, he lost interest in modern constructions. His view of architecture was determined by the idea that it had to be applicable in its country of origin, translatable into its language, in short, that it had to be useful.

He compared the role of the architect to that of the priest, demanding that the artist put all the force of his work at the disposal of his "people." This ethical position is equaled in its extremism only by that of Adolf Loos, whose missionary zeal was nonetheless tempered by his irony. Plečnik's ethical position, joined with his feelings of national duty and a deep religiosity, form the basis for his irreproachably honest confrontation with the phenomena of historicism and the modern movement. If, in 1930, Josef Frank was able to write "our times embody all historical times known to us," it was at the turn of the century that Jože Plečnik put this thought into practice in his architecture. His Arcadia, without a doubt, was Italy, his reference ancient Rome, the Renaissance, and, later on, even the baroque of his homeland; but he was also a realist, a practical man, able to update these experiences and historical creations and modify them according to his needs.

Whereas Adolf Loos explored the confines of architectural languages—down to the dialectical use of silence—Plečnik exposed himself to the diversity of languages and to the ambivalence of architectural semantics. His work reveals an attempt to transpose what he deemed to be the essential elements of the Western humanist tradition into a national Slovenian culture, an attempt bolstered by the dialectic between "popular" and "noble" cultures.

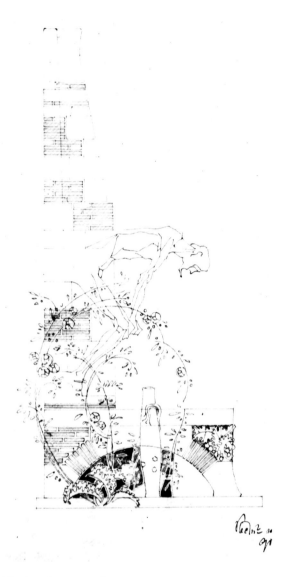

Design for a mural with fountain for the Secession exhibition of 1902

Yet it would probably be false to consider this rather late phase to be his particular contribution to the modern movement. In every phase of his life Plečnik sought "total architecture." A particular problem may have taken precedence on occasion, but the scope of his thought remained broad at all times; broader, in any case, than that of his Secessionist friends or of the city of his birth, Ljubljana, which never questioned its cultural identity. Therein lies the often apparent heterogeneity of his constructions, devoid of any doctrinaire purism, as well as of any obvious formal unity.

If Jože Plečnik has remained a practically unknown architect outside of his domain of Central European activities—in Vienna, Prague, and Ljubljana—it is due to the obstinate single-mindedness with which the history of the modern movement has been written, as well as to the anchorage of his work in a "cultural province" and to the impossibility of fitting this work into the flow of twentieth-century architecture. His distance from the problems and solutions of the modern movement make it difficult both to approach and to define his work. Whereas in the eyes of the avant-garde school he must have seemed desperately outdated in his stubborn reliance on the humanist tradition, for conservative schools he displayed a radicalism and eccentricity that strayed too far from the beaten paths. Paradoxical as it may seem, he even appeared too modern and unconventional. Despite his surface eclecticism, Plečnik was always an antieclectic; his choices in the interpretation of tradition were never arbitrary, nor merely those of a "follower."

One could claim that Plečnik adopted a kind of postmodern attitude regarding historicism and the modern movement, but he was much more radical, much more adventurous and reckless than any of today's postmodernists. His current rediscovery worldwide carries the same danger of being falsely interpreted as does Adolf Loos and his Chicago Tribune Tower. Plečnik's marginality with respect to the modern movement and his fascinating readability may lead critics to classify him among the predecessors of the postmodern movement, yet this could only occur under very particular conditions. Plečnik has neither the intellectualism nor the light touch of the postmodernists; he never sought to distance himself from things by use of irony or cynicism. He did not "quote" expressly, and when he did it was from memory and while integrating his quote into a constraining whole. Plečnik did not look to history for a means to distinguish himself from the present; for him history was the present. He did not have, or did not put into practice, a temporal concept of the West. All ideas were inscribed in the present, at the moment they were produced, no matter how ancient these ideas may have been. In this sense, Plečnik was an Oriental, like Josef Frank.

Plečnik's work also seems a challenge to our concepts of realism and regionalism. As Prelovšek aptly demonstrated,[1] Plečnik took Otto Wagner's doctrine according to which all things must have a function very seriously, endowing it with a spiritual, global sense. He thereby saved it from a superficial functional rationalism, like that found, fixed in an incurable formalism, in the galaxy surrounding Otto Wagner. His elaboration of the social, cultural, and political situation could even be called "realist," in the Marxist sense of the word, if it were not based on very different principles. Plečnik's attempt to adapt forms to their cultural frame of reference has more to do with common practicality than any of the attempts made by orthodox functionalists. Similarly, Plečnik provides a provocative and up-to-date response to the question of regionalism: he defined his architecture beginning with the dialectic of the periphery and the center, in each case deciding where to place the center. The provinces appear as a self-conscious world charged with positive value, a world that can counteract the center, and that should not be measured by the same yardstick. Regionalism thus becomes the articulation of a region starting with its center and is a challenge from the center.

In certain respects, it is therefore possible to compare Jože Plečnik to Antonio Gaudi. Like Gaudi, he inhabits a frontier zone between cultures; he is an "architectural fundamentalist," but also an artisan, a technician, an inventor, and a landmark figure for a newly developed national architecture. In his work, he was always fully conscious of his ethnic group and his region, while remaining critical with respect to "popular" as well as "noble" culture, and even able, through an extreme self-control, to integrate emotional phenomena such as kitsch into his field of reference.

With his conflicts, his temporal swings, his dialects and noble tongues, his linguistic consciousness and sensitivity, and the diversity of the sites and regions of his work, Jože Plečnik is the architect of Central European cultures that both overlap and divide at their borders. Perhaps we can explain Plečnik by way of the center, but we can understand him only by way of the periphery.

■ Note

1. Damjan Prelovšek, *Josef Plečnik, Wiener Arbeiten von. 1896 bis 1914* (Vienna, 1979).

Jože Plečnik and the Ljubljana Museum of Architecture

Petr Krečič

Ever since art historian Izidor Cankar wrote his critique of the Church of the Holy Spirit in Vienna in 1913, Plečnik has continued to draw attention from architectural historians and commentators alike. Between the two world wars he was the object of a polemic between modernist architects—who faulted him for his use of a historical vocabulary—and his supporters (such as France Stelè), who looked beyond this reproach and focused principally on the quality, the maturity, and the convincing and deeply spiritual content of his creations. After the Second World War, the focal point of studies began to shift. The critics were confronted with a fundamental question: in what way is Plečnik contemporary, despite the fundamental historicism associated with his modern forms and in light of his remaining at the center of thought at the Ljubljana School of Architecture? His successors, at least at the school, continued to insist on his centrality, which has never been denied. A second question also arose: how can Plečnik be explained in the context of the modern movement, his eclecticism being clearly opposed to the thesis of modern art, which defines itself through the radical rejection of all that is historical? At the time, this allowed for two answers: some said that he could be explained only in relation to his own work, that he was, therefore, beyond comparison, an unquestionable genius; others claimed that his formal world was not "usable" since it was impossible to draw upon it for the needs of current construction. But the evolution of architectural creation proved correct those who sought to unearth the concepts hidden beneath columns, arches, cornices, and other historical forms; those, then, who accepted his modern idea of the *self-generation* of forms, of their transformation and their combination, and who used this knowledge productively in dealing with forms in architecture and contemporary urbanism. The pioneering work done by Plečnik allowed many of his disciples, notably in the past thirty or forty years, to use a formal language that is recognizable, characteristic, original, and of generally high quality.

This stage of evaluation was followed by a theoretical and critical one, which at first was fairly ill-defined. It was the 1968 exhibition of Plečnik's work at the National Gallery (Narodna Galerija) that allowed us to rethink the role Plečnik had played in the evolution of Slovenian architecture. The event also drew attention to the insufficient technical means available for studying Plečnik's life and work, as well as for studying the history of architecture in general and of this century in particular. The Society of Architectural Critics, founded during the same period, was keenly aware of this lack and decided to create a museum of architecture, intended as a center for documentation and for the study of Slovenian architecture, past and present. The project benefited from a propitious circumstance: the availability of the Plečnik house in Trnovo (now incorporated into Ljubljana), containing the furniture and objects he used as well as his very rich archives of sketches, plans, models, photographs, correspondence, and more. Since Plečnik's death, his nephew, Father Karel Matkovič, had been administering the estate. With the help of Lojze Gostiša and of art history students, he had begun to organize the materials. At the time,

Gostiša persuaded Matkovič to bequeath the whole of Plečnik's estate to the city of Ljubljana. Upon Matkovič's death in 1970, the idea for an architecture museum coincided with that of a museum specially dedicated to Plečnik, an idea shared by his former students. It was Stane Bernik, one of the advocates of the idea of an architecture museum, who managed to bring this dream to life. Bernik was then president of the Cultural Committee of the city of Ljubljana as well as director of an art review, *Sinteza* (which is still published). The first documents necessary for the creation of the museum were drafted. Its statutes defined it as an independent institution that would choose, preserve, study, and present materials from several domains: architecture, urbanism, industrial aesthetics and design, and photography; an institution charged, among other things, with preserving and studying the collection of Jože Plečnik.

The museum's activities began in January 1972, marking the one hundredth anniversary of the architect's birth, with limited financial means and only two full-time employees. That same year it became home to the offices of the Biennale of Industrial Creation, still located there. It was understandably difficult to put the museum's ambitious program into practice. First because the small staff grew only very slowly; then because the available space, that of the Plečnik house, was modest in dimensions; finally, and most important, because the museum did not have—and still does not have—its own exhibition space. It was also difficult to treat architecture and urbanism in the same manner that objects typically destined for preservation and exhibition are treated; these two disciplines in a sense defy museographical arrangement.

From this perspective, it was easier to deal with the graphic art objects. Presenting Plečnik's own collection was not without its difficulties either, given the heterogeneity and the complexity of the material. As for the part of the archives that included sketches, plans, and models, much time was needed to examine, classify, and preserve them in proper conditions.

We have reconstructed the environment in which Plečnik lived—his bedroom, living room, studios, and their entrances—according to photographs taken immediately after his death. The museum published a guide to the collection to inaugurate its opening to the public in the spring of 1974, including a text by Plečnik specialist Damjan Prelovšek. Over the years, our collection of industrial and design objects has grown; large numbers of documents and books left by architects upon their death were bequeathed to the museum. Among these is a collection of plans and documents belonging to Ivan Vurnik (a friend of Plečnik at the architecture school of Ljubljana and a member of the famous *troika* that promoted modern architecture in Slovenia—Max Fabiani, Jože Plečnik, Ivan Vurnik—as well as that of Ivo Spinčič, a supporter of the rather radical wing of Slovenian functionalism.

But let us return to Plečnik. This modest, quiet man created so much during his life that even those who work at the museum and are in constant contact with his body of work are frequently surprised to discover new projects and to find new details concerning his life, work, and thoughts. The museum has become one of the most important sources of documentation for the study of Plečnik's work, especially since we systematically collect all that has been written and published about him. Researchers, journalists, and critics often come to us, not only concerning Plečnik, but with questions regarding Slovenian or Yugoslavian aesthetics or historical or contemporary architecture, as we are the only institution of its kind in the country. In short, all presentations of Plečnik's work lead to the museum.

The museum is located in a quiet quarter of Trnovo, not far from the center of town. Every attempt has been made to preserve the atmosphere of the architect's home much as he left it in January 1957. The site now has the somewhat "polished" look of a museum: the hustle and bustle that surrounded the master is gone; smells from his kitchen no longer drift through the house; his old friends are no longer heard at the door. But a visitor cannot help but feel the powerful spirit that shaped the rotunda, built next to the old house, containing furniture and numerous trinkets that had been given to him as gifts out of respect and affection. One cannot fully understand Plečnik in Ljubljana without seeing his modest and intimate home, his private world, and the incomparable antithesis of the monuments that follow, one after the next, once outside the house.

Professor Plečnik

Edo Ravnikar

Jože Plečnik was one of Slovenia's three or four most important contributors to the architecture and culture of this former Austro-Hungarian monarchy at the beginning of the century, and probably the most inventive among them. His life's journey began in a modest middle-class home, the class that made up the many small nations that in turn comprised the monarchy: a middle class characterized by mediocre education and little chance of social advancement. As a child he lived in a suburb of Ljubljana, a neighborhood of abundant vegetation, gardens, and only a few buildings, among which figured his father's woodworking shop, the studio of what we would today call a "small business-man." The religious and moral atmosphere that reigned in the family (Plečnik said of his parents that they were saints) was mostly due to his mother: she gave her first son to the church, as did her daughter later on. This generous family atmosphere was probably the source of the enthusiasm and altruism displayed by Plečnik throughout his life. A concern for others and an interest in their development were later to become the essential ingredients in his teaching.

His enrollment in a vocational school at the age of fourteen was his first step toward the architectural profession, a profession he did not have in mind at the start. A promising draftsman, he and a few fellow students were sent to a recently opened technical school in Graz modeled after the English system. Here he met his first true master, the architect Theyer, who befriended him and helped him become an exemplary architectural assistant. Plečnik worked evenings in the school's studio, where Theyer taught him the arcana of drawing. Theyer had an abundance of work and was in need of good draftsmen; he hired Plečnik and paid him a small salary.

This initial experience working for Theyer, in which practice was combined with theory, gave Plečnik a concept of pedagogy he would preserve throughout his life. The nature of the master-student relationship led him to strongly prefer practice over theory (traditionally, this demanding system has always been favored, from Leonardo to Le Corbusier, and we are returning to it today). It was this method he applied much later in teaching architecture students, both in Prague and Ljubljana.

Plečnik had neither the proper qualifications nor sufficient knowledge of mathematics and physics to exercise a serious pedagogical activity. Yet he had something rare and essential: a great sensitivity and a quick spirit, qualities that transcend pure intellect and the mastery of conventional knowledge. There is little theoretical reflection in his writings, and though we may find some in the letters of his youth, his final publications contain only what is necessary to support his drawings. His teaching was essentially visual, "artistic." In a letter from Italy he expressed his belief that the language of forms must take precedence over that of words.

Plečnik became the "popular" candidate upon Wagner's resignation in 1912, but his candidacy was not accepted. It was not the "č" of his name that was at fault, but his modest national

origin. In Wagner's studio and at the school, a split between the "upper" and "lower" social classes existed, each possessing its own ideology. The "superior" levels of society upheld Semper's views, which were tied in with power, the upper classes, the court, the academies, and with well-known architects. Although Wagner himself never took a stand, Semper's influence was present in Wagner's circle and formed a gulf between those who were "on top," such as Olbrich, Hoffmann, Bauer, and Fabiani, and the others: Plečnik, Kotěra, Kovačič, and Kastelic. With the construction of the Zacherl house, internal tensions grew, affecting Plečnik and in some ways changing him. This situation lasted throughout the struggle for Wagner's succession and ended only with Plečnik's departure for Prague, at which point he completely alienated himself from Wagner's circle. What Plečnik believed he could bring to the Secession, he now decided to bring to religious art. Abandoning furniture design, he began incorporating Ruskin's and Morris's wealth of ideas on decoration, architecture, and urbanism into his work. Thus, in the religious domain, he made use of their perspectives on Egypt, on Gothic art, and on early Christian art. He remained skeptical of classicism, except for the "revivals" he discovered in the work of Michelangelo, Vignola, and Palladio, such as the active form of the column, particularly the Ionic column in its many variations; the study of the classical tympanum; the relationship between architecture, climate, and materials; the will that animates the form; the collective work of art; the use of the square.

It seems that Ruskin's "subversiveness" was so in accordance with Plečnik's state of mind that his similarities—both in character and behavior—with the former, fifty years his elder,

happened of their own accord. Plečnik, whom
we can include among the architects of the Arts
and Crafts movement, was determined to find
inspiration in Ruskin and Morris, in the midst
of a Semper-oriented society. Thus, like the
ideas of Ruskin propagated through books and
through Gaudi-style gothic art, Plečnik's ideas
on organic architecture, on a different style of
painting, on moral norms and communism are
all directed against Semper's doctrines, to
which Wagner conformed, moreover, until the
end. Before the end of his stay in his beloved
Vienna, Plečnik had been transformed by the
principles of Ruskin and Morris and was able to
use this new knowledge as a teacher in Prague.

Pedagogically, Plečnik was a pantocrat, following the doctrine "have no other god but me":
creative docility and patient training were
required before the student could become independent. Plečnik was a pedagogue at heart, as
was Ruskin, and this elevated both of them
above the ordinary. It is impossible to know
what the Viennese Academy would have gained
had he stayed, or what it might have become
under his direction. It was in Prague, and then
in Ljubljana, that he was able to satisfy his need
to teach. His work is linked to his development
as a teacher, and even today continues its pedagogical mission.

**Plečnik and his
students traveling
in 1928**

CAREER

Plečnik, Vienna, and the Arcana of the Baroque Tradition

Alain Arvois

Cristina Conrad
von Eybesfeld

And as the same city regarded from different sides appears entirely different, and is, as it were, multiplied respectively, so, because of the infinite number of simple substances, there is a similar infinite number of universes that are, nevertheless, only the aspects of a single one as seen from the special point of view of each monad. (Leibniz, Monadology*)*

Jože Plečnik, a name that sounds loud and clear, a name, in turn, that echoes with the memory of that MittelEuropa of which Vienna was the focal point and the radiating center.

Plečnik was an architect to the core, in all the acts that, in the course of his life, determined a body of knowledge, a practice and a profession, but also and primarily a culture. A culture, that is, beyond the increasingly intensified opposition between culture and civilization,[1] the form itself of a tradition functioning as a tradition of form.

It is by attempting to return to this more refined and historical understanding of the *Bildung* tradition that the exact scope, the exact lesson, and the extreme knowledge of Plečnik's architecture can be understood. This *Bildung* tradition set into place a certain number of conditions and possibilities "that were realized in Plečnik's architecture, just as they gave weight at the time to the architecture of the 'Wagnerschule.'" Because they belong to this same tradition, we think that Plečnik and the Wagnerschule were in fact inseparable and that Plečnik was not the "author" of a unique architecture. His importance rests precisely on this fact, yet this is not the least of the paradoxes we will discover in his work.

Indeed, in architecture, despite the recent body of historiographic criticism that reduces its scope, the "author-function" marked the importance of a unique and unstable place where proof of a new stylistic grammar was initiated, a grammar that displaced the symbolic codes of architectural expression and reorganized them according to other paradigms. Within this movement, which we most often signify by names—authors' names—a new system of representation in architecture was founded, as if, as Gilles Deleuze assures us, "to found is always to found representation."

In this sense, we cannot consider Plečnik to be the author of an original and seminal architectural body of work, one that would be a turning point in the history of forms and that would inaugurate a new style in architecture. We are in Vienna and, to use a musical metaphor, we might say that Plečnik is a virtuoso interpreter, the composer of perfectly harmonious forms, but certainly not the author in architecture of a new type of orchestral writing. Rather, he was the author of an architecture that was "already there," present in the movement of the times and present first in Vienna, its center of crystallization. It is Vienna that determines Plečnik's architecture, and it is Vienna as "Capital City of the Empire" that must be considered its true author.

"There is a similar infinite number of universes that are, nevertheless, only the aspects of a single one as seen from the special point of view of each monad." The understanding of Plečnik's architecture also depends on this Leibnizian principle. Vienna, the empire, the Wagnerschule, but also, and especially, the baroque tradition: these must be viewed as an ensemble, not to deny Plečnik's personality, identity, and name, but to better grasp the extreme integrity, quality, and depth of his work. Without falling into "Vienna fin-de-siècle" stereotypes, we should first retrace the *circles of tradition* that orient Plečnik's architecture.

Vienna, the Empire, and the *Bildung* Tradition

Despite the at times facile derision with which the Austrian monarchy was regarded during the fin-de-siècle *stimmung,* it continued to maintain astonishing power. It was able to include gifted children from every level of the empire, from the farthest provinces and the poorest social classes, in a demanding and rigorous educational system. This extremely complicated, diversified policy of education taught absolute respect for the monarchy and religion—the tutelary powers—but also taught all the historical expressions of culture. It was in teaching and education—both expressions of the *Bildung*—that the state presented and represented itself; no other state has so linked the harmonious circle of its continuation to a policy of culture and education.

Within the perspective of a philosophy of history, it is of Hapsburg Vienna that Jacob Burckhardt is thinking when he singles out the powers of the *Geist* that form history and ensure its propagation. Thus, according to

Burckhardt, the spiritual powers at work in the historical world hinge on the three major spheres of state, religion, and culture. The two first principles of the state and of religion are stable structural elements that are beyond questioning. The third circle, that of culture, is the only one to express the creative aspect of the spirit, and it is through this circle that progress is made.[2]

But this triad of the state, religion, and culture is itself a repetition of the Leibnizian theory of preestablished harmony, which forms the most essential and most effective baroque paradigm of the monarchist tradition,[3] the arcana of its domination.

This very precise delimitation of modernity, initiated by the Age of Enlightenment, this very precise reduction of the *Aufklärung* to the sphere of culture, sets the stage for the *Bildung* that alone permits us to understand the continuity of the monarchy and the long-lasting consensus it obtained. In this *Bildung* a particular image of the social bond is founded, a self-representation of the community expressed in the outpouring of art and culture. This societal expression of the baroque tradition is so constructed that it achieves a sense of community through communion in aesthetic sentiment. From S. Zweig and Broch to Musil and Hoffmanstahl, all Viennese writers bear witness to this tradition, which persists in fin-de-siècle modernity. This is why, when the monarchy was contested, it was never according to the political tradition inherited from the *Aufklärung,* in the judicial sphere for example; instead, to be politically meaningful, the consensus had to be broken in the sphere of aesthetic values.

In the meantime, this scene of the *Bildung,* which was a prominent scene for state action, underwent a real and profound modernization in its educational system, granting the "humanities," and more broadly the "fine arts system," an essential function in the formation of a *sensus communis.*

Beginning in 1850, the empire established one of the most original educational systems in Europe, entirely oriented toward the assimilation of tradition, the "humanities," and cultural works. It combined a literary education with "applied arts" for example, unlike France, which still separates the two. This educational system strongly influenced Plečnik and was responsible for the extremely high technical quality of his architecture as well as that of the Wagner-schule: both are highly *cultivated* architectures.

It is therefore useful to remember that a certain cultural tradition, committed to an educational system that was constantly adapted and re-formed, notably by Bonitz and Count Thun,[4] was in turn deeply involved in the political tradition of the Hapsburgs, precisely in its baroque "destiny." This is why we recalled the exquisite sensibility of this paradoxical policy, a policy that was baroque in its tradition, using the Leibnizian philosophy of preestablished harmony as its tool, from "Josephism" to "Biedermeier" right down to Franz Joseph's Vienna. None of the Viennese singularity in artistic expression can be truly grasped if the tradition is not placed within the context of this program, leading us to enumerate a system of aesthetic references according to an incorrect version of history.

We cannot here retrace all of this tradition, which formed a political, aesthetic, symbolic, and imaginary space profoundly different in its possibilities from its French counterpart; on this point, one should consult the work by William

Johnston, *The Austrian Mind,* which in our opinion made its most valuable contribution by recalling this Leibnizian tradition of harmony. This book provides the latest synthesis of the Leibnizian tradition, that of Zimmermann, the official philosopher of the regime, who was influential in late-nineteenth-century academic reforms: "Zimmermann's most astounding doctrine," Johnston tell us,

was his interpretation of all human activities as being part of one of three forms of art. First came the art of education (Bildung kunst), *which brings the individual ideas and stimulation. Second, the art of images* (Bilde kunst), *which consists of bringing ideas and stimulation to others. Beginning with pedagogy, he worked his way up to social philosophy and the art of governing* (Staatskunst). *Finally, the plastic arts* (Bildende kunst) *consist in discovering and in recreating ideas in matter.*[5]

Johnston adds that "Zimmermann never failed to emphasize the continuity between knowledge, daily life, and the fine arts." Rather, "he saw all mental and practical activities as subdivisions of a single and immense quest called art."[6]

This "doctrine of knowledge" fully certifies the permanence of a tradition, for, in the triad composed of the art of education, the art of governing, and the plastic arts, we find, expressed by Zimmermann, *the arcana of the Hapsburgs' political tradition in its baroque paradigm.* It was a tradition that had a great capacity to captivate and orient the forces of culture and to integrate them in a communal whole. By deploying these forces in a certain direction—whether music, writing, theater, or architecture—this tradition activates, without changing them, the historical elements of structural stability—the state and religion. Nothing in Zimmermann's doctrine contradicts Plečnik's ethics or the "art of architecture" at the Wagnerschule.

Vienna as *Experimentum Mundi*

Having reconstructed the circles of a tradition, we now arrive at its center of gravity. It is in Vienna that the baroque tradition of the Hapsburg era was developed, experimented upon, and put into practice, before it spread, in turn, to the other regional capitals of the empire.

In order to be able to integrate a multiplicity of different nationalities and idioms, traditions and histories—to make them "possible together," in Leibnizian terms—the empire had to verify the syncretic capacity of a unified symbolism in its own capital, and this particularly in the domains of art and culture.[7] For these processes the Leibnizian theory of harmony, due to the multiple points of view and styles it legitimizes, was an excellent tool, making the so-called eclecticism or historicism of the Viennese a source of a novelty that was never in conflict with the historical and temporal order of the tradition with which the empire identified.

It was therefore up to Vienna, capital of the empire, to elaborate this synthesis, to verify its possibilities, and to send out an image to all points of the empire[8] of the symbolic, imaginary concept of communal integration, successfully reaching beyond the plurality of languages and idiomatic differences.

As such, it was in Vienna that the empire's unity was "acted out," presenting itself as the will for and the representation of the various aesthetics. This "representative" function of Vienna was magnificently perceived by Hermann Broch, who rigorously set out the reasons why Vienna was not, and would never be, a world metropolis.

The world is not its sphere, its dimensions are first that of the empire: *Öster Reich.* This *capital city,* in order to centralize its powers and decision making, must define the general contours of a consensus, of a cultural hegemony that will enable the empire to exist. Thus, Broch writes:

While Paris was coming to the end of its baroque structure, thus allowing it to blossom into the world city already germinating, Vienna remained a city of the baroque century. . . . Vienna became the city-that-is-not-a-world-metropolis; without ever becoming a small city, it sought the calm of a small city, the joys of a small city, the charms of yesteryear. It was still a metropolis, but a metropolis of the baroque century, the politics of which no longer existed.[9]

While for Vienna the politics of the baroque century no longer existed, in the sense of the territorial expansion of the empire, what historically characterized this political tradition remained—powerfully active, though perhaps in a manner that was hidden from itself: the influence of form and of the *Bildung* on the ensemble of cultural works. It was the tradition of form of which Vienna remained *l'experimentum mundi.*

Plečnik and the Wagnerschule

We have now outlined the general scheme of circles and orbits that *make up a system and its gravity*: the circle of culture and education, the circle of art and the state, and, finally, the circle that encompasses them in a *cosmography* and leads them to the *universality of the baroque tradition of preestablished harmony.*[10] The focal points chosen for these circles and their ellipses are Vienna and the empire, which together determined their historical and temporal trajectories. Within the three harmonic circles of

culture (*Bildung*), art (*Kunst*), and state (*Staat*) gravitate a multiplicity of "monads" that were like "so many different universes. One of them is minor within the system, but major with regard to the art of architecture in its "modern evolution": the Wagnerschule. In discussing it, we will have assembled all the conditions necessary for the interpretation—the hermeneutics, as it were—of Plečnik's architecture.[11]

Like all "monads," the Wagnerschule repeats the general order, of which it expresses the harmonic principles of circularity: it therefore includes an *art of educating in the art of the form that is the art of architecture.* As such, no discord can arise; the *Staatskunst* already comprises the Wagnerschule as one of its many possibilities. It is within such a framework that Plečnik gained his architectural knowledge: a framework whose authority and influence he recognized and whose guiding principles he accepted, and in which he himself had his roots. The initial influence of this educational tradition on Plečnik can now be examined more closely, allowing us to evaluate its lasting effects.

First, the *Bildung* tradition: Plečnik owes his formation to this tradition. After failing at the university, he entered the woodworking section of the Gradec Technical School. There he became a consummate draftsman and a craftsman; in the alliance between art and technical skills he would be able to receive training as an architect. Once he had been shaped by this tradition, he knew it was up to him, in turn, to "shape" it: to perpetuate its legacy by infusing his work with a tone that, while current and modern, *would remain faithful to the artistic, cultural, and social ideals of the baroque tradition.*

Second, the tradition of art as a concrete expression of social unity: It is the architect's duty to affirm the legitimacy of this idea. The architect must establish the good, for the good and the beautiful share a common destiny.

**Otto Wagner,
competition project
for the Berlin
Cathedral,** 1891

To this end, he must, as organizer, enlist the
cooperation of as many of the trades as possible.
The architectural (but also harmonic) mission of
the architect is to *maintain the working dignity* of
all social groups involved in construction and
threatened by industry.

Art and technique fuse only where the architect
assures that they are close and intertwined. The
tradition, therefore, of crafts, with its many
metalworkers, engravers, ceramists, stucco
workers, and carpenters can be maintained
within the complex and diversified harmony of
the architectural work only by a rejection of
modernity's "principle of economy," which de-
stroys the very essence of art. All of Plečnik's
architectural works are an expression of this

determined wholeness. Entirely designed, shaped, constructed, and labored upon, right down to the nonvisible parts, his works are always *microcosms that incorporate and model all the materials the universe has to offer.*

Third, the tradition of a redeeming art: Whatever the motto—"*Artis sola domina necessitas*" (in the Semper version), or "Art lifting the veil that always weighed upon humanity" (in the later Wagner version), or even, according to the motto placed on the pediment of the "temple of art and religion" erected by Olbrich for the Secession, "*Der Zeit ihre kunst, der kunst ihre freiheit*"—the tradition of a redeeming art aims at maintaining the essential baroque paradigm with respect to culture and politics, which, in 1882, was still being proclaimed by the philosopher Zimmermann.[12]

Three great traditions, therefore, constantly form and intertwine in Plečnik's works. But these traditions, once guidelines for the work of architecture, were, at the end of the century, questioned in the name of *modernity,* or *Neuzeit.*

When, in 1894, Plečnik entered Otto Wagner's studio, the latter had just been appointed professor at one of the two special schools of architecture created by the Academy of Fine Arts in Vienna. Wagner's inaugural lesson, which he delivered in 1894 and restated in his *Modern Architecture,* grants the "functionalist" themes of Gottfried Semper a certain primacy, thus placing "the artistic intentions" of the architectural work in perspective. Modernity makes its appearance at the Wagnerschule in the form of a question: Which is primary, form or technique, tradition or innovation?

But it is important to consider that *the quest for modernity,* repeatedly addressed in Wagner's *Modern Architecture,* does not coincide with

the more fundamental opposition that gives it meaning and that was played out on the university scene between Alois Riegl and Semper.[13]

In affirming the autonomy of artistic forms in their "will to speak," Riegl's *Kunstwollen* stands in opposition to the historical determinism of material civilization, supported by Semper in the evolution of artistic forms. Around the year 1900, this debate found significant political expression in Viennese architecture.[14]

It would be tempting to draw a parallel between the opposition, in architecture and urban planning, of Riegl and Semper, on the one hand, and Sitte and Wagner on the other. But oppositions in Vienna tend to synthesize, opening new paths, and can never remain in purely logical and contrary positions. An intercessor always steps in who readdresses the conflict and resolves the opposition with a concrete artistic solution that would be attributed to some universal wisdom, to the desire to perpetuate *Gemütlichkeit*—an untranslatable Viennese term that signifies a "well-being" that risks being threatened and disturbed by any conflict—or to an enlightened conservatism that would have incorporated Guépard's motto "everything must change in order to remain the same."

We will attribute it to the imperial doctrine of preestablished harmony, of which Wagner was, in the domain of architecture, the leading representative. For, in fact, between Riegl and Semper, between Sitte and Wagner, the debate was restricted to the dialectic *traditio/innovatio* and to the sole discussion of the *respective primacy* of these terms in the sphere of art.[15]

For Riegl, art as a tradition comes first and foremost from memory, and artistic innovation must combine with memory in order to avoid the ever-present risk of its effacement. Hence, for example, the extraordinary dialectic used by Riegl in *Le Culte moderne du monument*[16] between the monument's "ancient values" and its "new values." These two systems have the greatest chance of being reconciled in religious art. There is no question that Plečnik was inspired by these analyses for his church and sacred architecture projects.

Although for Semper tradition still constitutes a "historical grammar of styles," it is unable to program innovation (unlike a universal language) from which the *Neuezeit* of modernity will arise. Other conditions are necessary for this innovation; namely, technical progress. But by this reference—*horresco referens*—to the autonomous powers of technology, the most important cause of architectural novelty, tradition itself may ultimately be endangered. More precisely, it is the relationship and the harmonious survival of the *traditio-innovatio* rapport that is threatened. We believe that one of the most profound structures of the Wagnerschule enabled it to avoid this threat and to maintain, on all architectural and urbanistic levels, the terms of the alliance.

Thus we should not overemphasize the opposition between Sitte and Wagner. Though it was real, it was not, in our view, fundamental. On this point we disagree with the adept analyses of Carl Schorske, who points to a return to Sitte and interprets it as a sign of Wagner's failure to live up to modernity: "Despite his will to avoid the cloistered mentality of Sitte, Wagner's growing awareness of the artist's isolation and his relative impotence to shape the modern world, even according to its own utilitarian needs, had forced him back upon the past he wished to leave behind."[17]

There is an even more fundamental reason why Sitte and Wagner cannot be so easily pitted against one another: beyond their respective modifications of each of the terms of the *traditio/innovatio* dialectic, *the idea of the city* remains, for each, *the regulating force, in the Kantian sense,* of all architectural and urban thought, and the object of their intentions. This is why it makes no sense to view Wagner as a theoretician of the metropolis, not only for the reasons stated by Hermann Broch—"Vienna will never be a world metropolis"—but because Wagner's study for a large city (*Die Groszstadt*) concerns Vienna and its extension within an urban framework that remains essentially baroque in its monumentality.

And both Sitte and Wagner were in absolute agreement on this primordial arcana: *the city is a work of total art.* This idea of the city as *Gesammstkunstwerk* is not only entirely integrated in the urban baroque tradition, but is even fundamental to it.[18] And it is here, once again, that the circle of the *Bildung* closes and defines the architectural culture of the Wagnerschule: Vienna, *the city in which and by which the baroque tradition survives.*

The baroque tradition of "form," of education, and of tradition as education are all manifestations of the *Bildung* and the *Kunst,* which together oriented Plečnik's architecture. Thus, beyond the specific stylist types such as Jugendstil or Secession, Plečnik's work leads us to consider the extraordinary permanence of the baroque tradition in the Wagnerschule. And, from the perspective of the baroque tradition, with its ensemble of aesthetic, ethical, historical, but also architectural and urban components that Vienna represents, *the architecture of Plečnik and that of the Wagnerschule are inseparable.*

Our circles are connected and can now be interpreted: *what characterizes Plečnik's architecture are his deep roots in the baroque tradition.* We have stressed the manner in which the stylistic traits of modernity used by Plečnik and the Wagnerschule were articulated upon the permanence of that tradition. The importance and intrinsic qualities of Plečnik's architecture lie in this articulation, in his strong and constant abilities; his teachings cannot be restricted to the conventional Jugendstil or Secession labels.

To avoid the conception of the baroque as a mere stylistic phenomenon, it was necessary to retrace its artistic and political aspects, notably at the points where art, culture, and the state conceived of themselves within a *political philosophy of history, culture, and the empire.* The result is a baroque paradigm that creates a unique framework of meaning and experience within which Plečnik's architecture must be viewed.

Everyone can journey at his own pace and discover in Plečnik's architecture the places and forms of a baroque permanence, following a path that in many respects should present itself as an "art of the past." But for this particular journey or promenade, we will nonetheless suggest an itinerary: one concerning Plečnik's architecture, the other his urban planning. Each aids, in its own way, an understanding of the significance of baroque architectural principles, such as they were reused and translated by Plečnik on two occasions: for the facade of the Zacherl house and in the urban restructuring of Ljubljana.

The Zacherl House and the Architectural Dignity of Facing

Baroque building technology in Austria employs a constant duality between simple, even rustic structural elements, mostly of brick, and a sophisticated, sumptuous decoration, principally of stucco, that covers the building materials. This construction principle is found in all civic buildings, from country homes to palaces and churches. Pierre Charpentrat notes that the great baroque architects Zimmermann and E. Q. Asam, are "stucco specialists."[19] In this building tradition, facing gives "form," fashions the facade, and makes it majestic. One need only consider the restoration work on any Austrian palace from the baroque era to appreciate the extreme simplicity and rusticity of the structure when its walls and windows are stripped of their ornamentation and to sense how much such an architecture, once it has recovered its sumptuous appearance, owes to the theater.

When, therefore, contrary to the most firmly stated precepts of the "Semper doctrine," the architects of the Wagnerschule dress their supporting structures in facing that, whatever shape it may take, *gives form and figure to the building,* they seem to be following the baroque tradition, with its tendency toward innovation. It is important to understand that the facing— stucco or majolica, gray marble, or granite slabs—should not be viewed as skin deep, a mere superficial addition, lightly "dressing" the facades of buildings to which the supporting system alone confers meaning and form. The facing *is* the facade, the presentation and the representation of the building, the structure of which is subordinate. This is one of the central traits of the Wagnerschule, attesting to its continuity with the baroque tradition, which was initially a *visible tradition.*

Such a view, if accepted, forces us to minimize the importance of Jugendstil or Secession iconography in Plečnik's architecture, or rather to place these within the *iconographic field of the baroque,* in order to grasp the *extraordinary depth* of the work of Plečnik and of the Wagnerschule. We can no longer speak of a "dialectic" between structure and facing, between form and content; form *is* content; dualities are overwhelmed by an effusive celebration of the symbolic materiality of the architecture.

This idea is superbly illustrated by the Zacherl house, truly Plečnik's masterpiece (see "Portfolio" section). Within this facade, the tension between baroque *tradition* and *innovatio* seems both to be taken to its *modern* limits and to be relieved. It is as it the demise of the baroque tradition were inscribed in this experiment with limits. And it is, indeed, inscribed. Look at the statue, which the facade appears to be casting off, a statue frozen in its fall, the sculpture of a body which the architecture no longer desires, a symbol of this loss and separation. An archangel on the facade, arms open in pure suspension, celebrates the enigma of visibility, and therefore of the baroque, once and for all.

The Urban Tradition of Counterpoint

The Zacherl house is also commendable for its integration into the old city, and thus its continuation of the urban tradition of the baroque *Bildung.*

To approach the other side of the urban culture of "large" forms, a side that emerges in history through the assured and respectful knowledge of "small" architectural forms, thus perpetuating the "contrapuntal" orchestration of the city, we suggest a second key for the reading of Plečnik's work.

This key concerns Plečnik's work in Ljubljana as part of a master plan to develop the old city, a plan laid out by Max Fabiani.[20] This plan will one day be studied as an example of one of the great works of late nineteenth-century culture. Its historical intelligence and the profound philosophical knowledge of the city manifested in all its parts make it a great work of the mind. It is within the framework of this plan that Plečnik initially acted; the whole of his urban planning must be analyzed to understand the concerted symphony of his urbanism.

We will focus on only one of these musical phrases, the redevelopment of the river that crosses and runs parallel to the old city. Among the incontestably gothic and baroque growth of its banks, which he treats as a major, sovereign space, Plečnik designs bridges of legendary beauty, outlines a network of small piazzas and quays, organizes quality urban "furnishings," and distributes fountains and statues, all in pure Secession style. But whoever travels these varied spaces, which have become the main promenades of the city, finds a deep unity between the baroque jewels of the facades and the "exhibition" of the Secession's architectural discourse, a unity due precisely to the strong differences in their individual stylistic expressions.

Here is an extreme architectural culture, vibrant and personal, a consummate art of counterpoint. Few examples exist of urban planning so affirmed in its own style, maintaining such coherence, resonance, and harmony with its baroque heritage. We can still enjoy today the experience of such an architectural offering, and in this gift lies Plečnik's extreme architectural probity. Baroque in its deep structure, contemporary on the surface, his architecture is stylistically of a period that contributed to the forming and shaping of beautiful objects; it introduces us to the *possibility of an emotional experience of the city.*

Ljubljana is the *lesson* of a demanding and rigorous architectural *innovatio,* deployed with a faithful respect for the urban *tradition* that formed and shaped it. It remains to be understood how such a lesson, such an experience which must be remembered and questioned again, can be irremediably lost to us. With this loss, another story begins: that of the modern movement, with its urban forerunners.

But as for Plečnik's architecture, it forces us to experience this paradox: that an architecture cannot be reduced to what it displays on the surface, that it cannot be explained by the codes at the time of its construction, and that, to participate in its long, rhythmic history, we must understand that in every architecture is a depth that gives it meaning, even though we may no longer be able to see it.

The *depth* of Plečnik's architecture and that of the Wagnerschule—a school we must one day call by its true name, the Wienerschule—is *the baroque tradition.* It was the *auctor* of Plečnik's architecture, with which we will now close our circle. If such depth remains hidden to our eyes—overly anxious to read the signs of the Viennese Secession—it should not surprise us, as long as we can still understand the *Witz* of that other Viennese, Hugo Van Hoffmannstahl, who wrote: "Depth? it has to be hidden. Where? on the surface."

■ Notes

1. See J. Starobinski, *Le temps de la reflexion* (Paris: Gallimard, 1983).

2. See Paul Ricoeur, *Temps et recit,* vol. 3 (Paris: LeSeuil, 1985), p. 340. It is worth noting that Nietzsche relentlessly philosophizes against such a theoretical approach to historical development in his critiques of *L'histoire antiquaire* and of the *Seconde Inactuelle.*

3. See Emile Boutroux's introduction to the *Monadology.*

4. Bonitz, a great Aristotelian if ever there was one; Count Thun, who caused Freud to have most peculiar dreams.

5. *The Austrian Mind: An Intellectual and Social History 1848–1938* (Berkeley: University of California Press, 1976). Here translated from the French edition, *L'Esprit viennois,* p. 336.

6. Ibid., p. 338.

7. A policy of the empire to which the liberals do not conform. Thus, the liberal leader J. Berger said in 1861: "The Germans in Austria should strive not for political hegemony, but for cultural hegemony among the peoples of Austria." Quoted in Carl E. Schorske, *Fin-de-Siècle Vienna: Politics and Culture* (New York: Alfred A. Knopf, 1980), p. 117 and p. 175 n. 2.

8. There was the Hapsburg dream and myth of a recreation of the Roman Germanic Saint Empire, a baroque dream that Y. Bonnefoy recalls in "L'Architecture baroque et son destin," in *L'Improbable* (Paris: Gallimard, 1984).

9. H. Broch, "Hoffmannstahl et son temps," in *Création littéraire et Connaissance* (Paris: Gallimard, 1966), p. 85.

10. See, on this subject, the important work by Claudio Magris, *Il mito asburgico nella letteratura austriaca moderna* (Turin: Einaudi), 1963.

11. We are, in fact, subscribing to a hermeneutics of art in this interpretation of Plečnik's architecture. See H. G. Gadamer, *Herméneutique ou l'art de comprendre* (Paris: Aubier, 1982).

12. Schorske made note of this aspect, yet without connecting it to the baroque tradition of the Hapsburgs in Vienna. He does a wonderful job of emphasizing that one of the members of the Secession explained "her commitment to the movement as 'a question of defending a purely Austrian culture, a form of art that would weld together all the characteristics of our multitude of constituent peoples into a new and proud unity,' what, in another place, she called a 'Kunstvolk' (an art people)." Berta Szeps-Zuckerkandl, quoted in Schorske, p. 237 and p. 295 n. 29.

13. A. H. Venturi retraces this theoretical debate between Semper and Riegl in *R. Zimmermann et les origines de la science de l'art*. It should be noted that Riegl was a student of Zimmermann, a representative of the Leibnizian tradition.

14. One of the best current works on Viennese architecture in 1900 is that of F. Borsi and E. Godoli, *Vienna 1900* (New York: Rizzoli, 1985), which accurately recreates the terms of this debate.

15. These two concepts were to split much later, thus giving rise to our modernity.

16. See the excellent introduction by Jacques Boulet on Riegl in "Le Culte moderne du monument," *In extens, U.P.* no. 1 (1985).

17. Schorske, pp. 109–110.

18. This notion of *Gesammstkunstwerk* is generally related to Richard Wagner's aesthetic and to opera, due to an anachronism already criticized by Nietzsche. It would be better to relate this conception to *the idea of the city* as it appeared in the Baroque and Renaissance periods.

19. P. Charpentrat, *Baroque* (Fribourg: Skira, 1964). See also Bonnefoy, "L'architecture baroque et la pensée du destin," in *L'Improbable*.

20. The urban work of Max Fabiani, which is little known, was the subject of a detailed study by M. Posetto and is extensively quoted in the excellent work by Borsi and E. Godoli, *Vienna 1900*.

The Life and Work of Jože Plečnik

Damjan Prelovšek

Jože Plečnik was born in Ljubljana, on January 23, 1872, the third child of a woodworker from Karst. Throughout his life he remained deeply marked by his familial environment, in which austerity, religiosity, and the love of work reigned. While one brother studied to become a priest and the other a doctor, Jože was destined to take over the family workshop.

Childhood and Education

During his first four years in primary school, Plečnik was also trained in the family trade of woodworking. He loved to draw, but his father opposed his desire to become a painter. From 1888 to 1892, he attended the woodworking section at the technical school in Graz, where he received a fellowship. He spent his Sundays and the hours after class drawing at the studio of his master, Léopold Theyer, who greatly appreciated his talent. Plečnik was too young to take over the family business when his father died, and he remained in Graz. With Theyer's help, he later went to Vienna, where for two years he designed furniture and supervised production for a large woodworking company. He tried unsuccessfully to enroll at the School of Decorative Arts and frequented museums, galleries, and exhibitions.

At the School of Otto Wagner

One Sunday afternoon at the Künstlerhaus, he happened upon Otto Wagner's plan for the new cathedral in Berlin. With no recommendation, he presented himself to Wagner, who accepted him into his studio for the school year 1894–95. In the autumn, while Plečnik was still hesitating between architecture and decorative arts, Wagner expressed his desire to take him on as a student, and from October 1895 to June 1898 Plečnik studied with Wagner at the Academy of Fine Arts. He became attached to his master as to a second father; he literally developed a passion for the Wagnerian architectural revolution, convinced that art could make a decisive contribution to the creation of a better world. His meeting with Wagner coincided with the most decisive period in the development of modern Viennese architecture, a time that called for a new aesthetic. Plečnik adhered wholeheartedly to the precepts of Wagner's book *Modern Architecture*. Another student, Joseph Hoffmann, was later to say of him, "He was completely absorbed by his work and his plans, and it was impossible to interest him in anything else. This inner concentration caused him to be very reserved, and he devoted himself entirely to his tasks."

Plečnik was closer to Wagner than most of his fellow students, as he earned his living by drawing in his master's studio four to five hours a day. Yet something powerful separated the student from his master. An idea that was entirely foreign to the cosmopolitan Wagner ran throughout Plečnik's reflections: the idea that true art is the fruit of hard labor, which implies suffering. Plečnik saw his new profession as a kind of Franciscan vow made to the Slovenian people. Unlike Wagner, who possessed broad architectural knowledge, Plečnik conceived his theories in moral terms, which remained at the heart of his subsequent research. Thus at first he was disappointed by his master's liberal

views on faith. Plečnik was equally bothered by the fact that Wagner gave preference to the technical aspects of architecture, as this did not correspond to his decidedly artistic nature. After traveling in the same direction for many years, there came a day when their paths quite naturally diverged.

The Plečnik family in 1889: his mother Helena, his father Andrej, and their children (left to right) Jože, Andrej, Janez, and Marija

Wagner's plastic language became especially distinct as he worked on plans for the Viennese metro. And Plečnik, who oversaw construction during its entire duration—from the beginning of 1894 until the inauguration of the final stop in the line on the brink of the twentieth century—participated in the birth of a new forms and thus learned their technical nature.

The Anker Insurance Building in Graben figures prominently among the works that opened the door to architecture for Plečnik. The facade contains all the elements characteristic of Wagner in his composition of commercial buildings: the treatment of the first two floors as a whole, the unified conception of the building, with decoration concentrated on a large cornice, and the vertical break in the facade. Wagner never modified his nineteenth-century style, but tried to modernize it by use of Semper's doctrine. The transformation of Viennese architecture is most apparent from the exterior. Wagner turned the building's facade into a flat surface, while favoring ornamentation as the precursor

Otto Wagner and his collaborators in 1898. Plečnik is the second from the right; behind him is Josef Hoffman; Joseph Maria Olbrich is first on the left.

of the new era. This is why draftsmen gifted with a rich imagination, such as Josef Maria Olbrich and Plečnik, were most welcome in his studio. While both had difficulty mastering the engineering aspect of architecture, Wagner appreciated their artistic talent. Olbrich and Plečnik became the pioneers of the new functional style (*NutzStil*) even though they were never counted among the most audacious engineers.

Thus, in 1895, even before Plečnik was skilled enough to complete a project of his own, Wagner took advantage of his talent as a decorator and assigned him work on the Neumann Department Store at the Kärntnerstrasse. Plečnik finished his first school year with plans drawn for the commercial building at 40 Linke Wienzeile, where Wagner's famous Majolika house was to be built three years later. In a letter to his mother for her birthday, in the spring of 1896, Plečnik speaks of his rapid progress.

During the summer of 1896, he most likely collaborated on the construction of the Gumpendorferstrasse station, and the following year on that of the Saint-John-of-Währing chapel. Judging by sketches of the Burggasse station preserved in Plečnik's archives, we can conclude that he was also involved in the final plans for the Gürtel metro line. It is difficult to precisely determine the extent to which Plečnik participated in Wagner's work: the latter generally sought the help of his best students. At times Plečnik's designs can be identified by his extraordinary mastery, his love of antique motifs, his unique handwriting, and the Slavic words he occasionally scattered among the titles. The skillfully drawn silhouettes on his plans are of simple people, whereas Olbrich preferred drawing elegant figures, adorned with touches of color. The commercial building at 38 Linke Wienzeile is among the buildings by Wagner in which Plečnik's participation is incontestable.

Study for a villa,
c. 1898

The young architect's designs for the portico, drawn at the beginning of November 1897, have been preserved. It was not the novelty of his forms, but the way in which they are used that enabled Plečnik to surpass his colleagues.

To be from Wagner's studio was quite an impressive credential at the time; when Plečnik struck out on his own, this reputation assured him work. He captured the public's interest at the beginning of 1898 with his project for the Gutenberg monument. Of forty-three proposals, the jury granted him one of two first prizes. Although the project was never realized, the competition caused somewhat of a commotion, for it was, so to speak, the Secession's first public victory in Vienna. Shortly afterward, the architect's name once again received public mention. The Association of Decorative Arts of Southern Austria asked Wagner to help design the premises in the Prater rotunda that had been selected for the Jubilee exhibition, and he entrusted the commission to his student, provided that Plečnik find a suitable solution. Plečnik used drapery to give the room an oval form and placed two great chandeliers in the center. Going against the current techniques and using only simple means, he arranged the exhibited objects into distinctive groups. Adolf Loos sang his praise, and Otto Wagner himself declared, "Even a classical architect, in his time, could not have found a better solution."

Plečnik completed his studies with one of the utopian projects that Wagner, following a practice common at the School of Fine Arts in Paris, introduced to Vienna to stimulate his students' imagination. Until then, Plečnik had not paid much attention to questions of urban planning. While preparing the project for his diploma on the development of a seaside resort in Scheveningen-on-the-Haag, he became interested in "Artibus," his master's old pet project that, despite its heavily historicist content, continued to pass for a summary of the classical principles of monumental urban construction. Despite its modern shell, the plan contains elements of buildings and historical sites appreciated in Wagner's circle. This is equally true of the two belvederes situated in front of the resort's main building, designed with considerable audacity and ingenuity, and also proving Plečnik's concept of sculpture as an organic element in architecture. During the preceding academic year, Wagner had been particularly occupied with sacred architecture, and it was probably Wagner's plans for a Capuchin monastery,

on which Plečnik directly participated, that oriented the latter more clearly toward the problematic question of contemporary churches, a question that preoccupied him his entire life.

Having received his diploma with honors (third in his class after Hoffmann and Kotěra), Plečnik won a stipend for travel to Rome and embarked on his journey at the beginning of November 1898.

Studies Abroad

During his travels, Plečnik viewed historical works with varied sentiments and states of mind: compared to classicism, modern architecture seemed more and more deficient. He also began to doubt certain of his master's solutions, though he continued to be firmly convinced of the correctness of his direction.

From Rome, in the spring of 1898, the architect announced to his brother Andrej that he had found a new manner for treating longitudinal churches. Yet he still had a long way to go before producing his first church, and his Italian experiments brought only partial improvement to his liturgical and aesthetic conceptions. Plečnik ended his Italian voyage in Rome. Tuscany and the eternal city gave him all he had dreamed of in Vienna: antiquity, the churches of the first Christians, Bramante, and especially Michelangelo and the late Renaissance period, in which he was particularly interested. He even became acquainted with the Vatican and was drawn to Mediterranean architecture. But henceforth he would choose his models according to his own taste.

From Rome he went to Spain, which he quickly left for France, and after a visit to Lourdes, arrived in Paris. He expected a great deal from the city's historical architecture and from the

**Rome sketchbooks,
study for a modern
church, 1899**

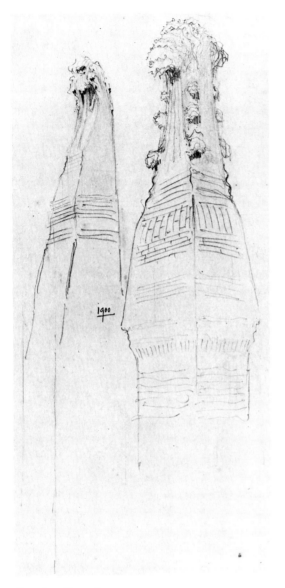

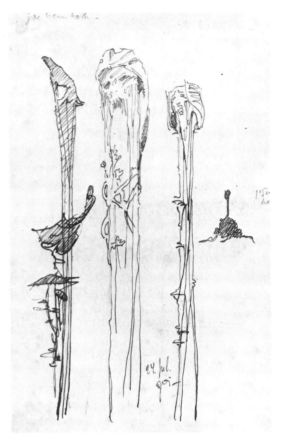

Sketches for a garden
fountain, 1901

Sketches for pylons,
1900

Architectural fantasy

Exposition Universelle, then in preparation. But coming from classical Italy, he was less well disposed toward the center of fin-de-siècle French novelty. Upon receiving news of his mother's death, he took a rapid tour of the principal monuments of Paris and shortened his voyage—even though his initial intention, following his master's advice, had been to visit several other European countries of artistic significance.

First Projects

Plečnik began working in Wagner's studio in the autumn of 1899 and remained there until the following summer. After Olbrich's departure for Darmstadt, he became the studio's most important artist. The knowledge gained during his travels had no decisive effect on his work during this period, for it was the time of the Secession's great effervescence in the artistic world. As we learn in a letter to the architect Jan Kotěra, Plečnik almost single-handedly conceived of the Rossauerlände and Schottenring stations for the metro line that runs alongside the Danube. Disturbed by the type of construction imposed, he nonetheless succeeded in producing a harmonious ensemble of streamlined forms. He used ornamentation almost exclusively inspired from historical styles, but in a proportion relative to the great surfaces of white roughcast plaster, giving the impression of an entirely modern architecture. On the visible parts of the metallic constructions, he weaves the vegetal decoration so characteristic of the Secession, carefully ensuring that the flowers do not remain merely ornamental and do not mask the development of the metallic supporting structure. Two drawings from this time show that Plečnik also worked with Wagner on the plans for the Modern Gallery of Vienna, a project that was never built.

Plečnik's Work in Vienna

An Independent Artist

Plečnik's opportunities for work, which were apparently very numerous in the beginning, became rarer and rarer. When his brother, Andrej, drew his attention to available jobs at home, Jože proudly resisted, convinced that Vienna was of vital importance for the development of his art. At first he tried to work with Wagner's son Otto on a project to renovate hotels in Varsovie, but he ended the association after noticing that the young Wagner ran up bills that were too high for his taste. As he wanted neither to return to the Slavic south nor to respond to the invitation from Varsovie nor to replace Kotěra in Prague, he was left with the status of an independent artist. His ties with the Secession, which he officially rejoined in 1901, gave him some hope for the future.

Leaving Wagner's Studio

Wagner was both protective and paternal toward his collaborators, and he bore Plečnik's periods of indecision with patience. More or less open conflict, however, did arise. In leaving Wagner's studio, Plečnik did not mean to burn his bridges, but in addition to financial interests, he anticipated greater contact with the contemporary art of Austria and abroad. In letters to Jan Kotěra, he regularly communicated his impressions of exhibitions held in the Olbrich Pavilion in Naschmarkt. When, at the

Langer house, Vienna,
1900–1

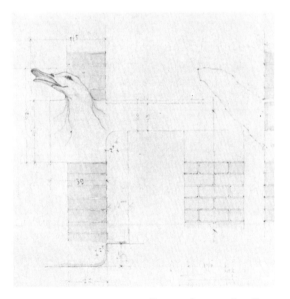

Langer house, details
of facade

beginning of the century, the Secession broke through its original framework and began to influence German and Belgian art, as well as modern French art, he enthusiastically wrote to Kotěra (January 1901):

I would like to draw your attention to the Secession: Segantini, Rodin——Frenchmen——and the Spaniard Zuloaga. Of course the crazy Klinger ruins this Olympian joy. Rodin's Bourgeois de Calais is indescribable. Segantini is the purest soul I have ever seen. The Spaniard is good at representing the weaknesses of his people. The French——the painters——are the substratum of painting, and one begins to think: Klinger's finished.

First Commissions

Plečnik was initially obliged to execute modest commissions. His renown as a furniture designer and decorator helped him find work, and he was careful to maintain his contacts at the master's studio. For the modernization of contractor Karl Langer's house in Hietzing, a suburb of Vienna, the young architect attempted to free himself of his master's influence. In the summer of 1901, with the foundations already laid, the owner asked Plečnik to design a new facade and to improve the interior layout. Plečnik used the subway stations of the period as inspiration for the interior, but for the facade he tried to avoid Wagner's rationalism, seeking inspiration in Belgian architecture instead. He also used Olbrich and Kolo Moser as models in many places, while imitating the Béranger manor house by Guimard for the facade's sculptures. This proved to be his most serious flirtation with fin-de-siècle style. Despite an evident heterogeneity of form, the gently undulating rhythm of the wall, which originates in the salon and fades in the axis of the kitchen window, dominates the facade of the Langer house. Plečnik covered the entire available surface of the facade with curves and stylized flowers, thus distancing himself from the ornamentation techniques used by Wagner for the Majolika.

The villa for the notary Loos in Melk on the Danube, undertaken with Josef Czastka, a colleague from Wagner's school, constituted a new, though less successful attempt at seeking a plastic language—one that would be both adapted to its times and liberated from trendy forms.

When he realized that he had not found a convincing response to the question of style, he once again turned to classic roughcast plaster and tried and true ornamentation, this time for a commercial building for Karl Langer, with whom he worked regularly at the time. Though it was practically impossible to create something new within the framework of the large barrack-style buildings common to Vienna, Plečnik proved his mastery. Solely by means of a very fine organization of the wall, he achieved an impression of equilibrium and incredible lightness. He found an equally good solution for

Loos house, Melk,
1901

Langer building,
Vienna, 1901–2

the liaison between the varying roof heights, and special note should be paid to the balconies that run along the corners, erasing distinct borders between the facades. To increase their lightness, he embellished these balconies with glass floors. He had apparently learned that it was best to avoid untried foreign models. The balconies, for example, were the result of a creative confrontation with the solutions by Wagner's circle. The vestibule and the staircases come as close as possible to rendering the desired impression.

Above all, Plečnik found this fin-de-siècle epoch to be a lyrical and colorful time, full of good humor, which he was able to render with precision, making almost exclusive use of the classical architectural vocabulary. Disappointed with the banality of the Secession, which had degenerated, he declared, as early as 1902, "I yelled—now I am no longer yelling; I search for myself wherever I happen to be. Like a spider, I aim to attach a thread to tradition, and beginning with that, to weave my own web."

The Biedermeier house, at the entry to Hietzing, transformed by Plečnik and Czastka in 1901 for a businessman, Josip Weidman, shows the architect's creative confusion in the period of transition. He designed an interesting street facade for the house, foreshadowing that of the Zacherl house. Yet in the course of construction, he allowed himself a few questionable references to Schönbrunn's baroque. The rear facade of the house and its furnishings were conceived in a very modern style, but did not appease his disappointment, as he claimed that he had not had enough time and was misunderstood. "Such a work will not sing the glories of its creator as it should, given the force within me, but nothing can be done."

Plečnik and Sacred Art

Sacred art began to attract Plečnik more and more. But as he developed this interest, the number of his clients diminished and he encountered widespread misunderstanding. For weeks at a time he studied and perfected projects for which it was practically impossible to earn any money. He wasted a great deal of time on a competition for the newly created artistic section at the Society of Léon in Austria and worked for two years on the designs for a holy sepulcher, in return for which he received only slight compensation. He was undoubtedly driven by a desire to free himself from the strong influence of his master, but even more from his attachment to his brother. At the Society of Léon Plečnik made the acquaintance of the court's prelate, Heinrich Swoboda, and of Johann Evangelist Zacherl, a manufacturer, who for a time aided Plečnik in warding off economic downfall. The architect expected support for his work from the highly placed Swoboda—who passed for an expert in matters of modern religious art—but Swoboda disappointed him: when he found himself in trouble because of the Church of the Holy Spirit, he was utterly alone.

Slovenian Nationality

To understand Plečnik, one must consider the national component of his architecture, that is, the network of ties with his country of birth, to which he became even more attached once he turned independent and which allowed him to safely navigate among the various artistic and philosophical currents of the time. In particular, it conditioned his choice to opt against German art or, more precisely, against Northern art, a choice that became especially noticeable after his move to Prague. In this regard, Plečnik also owed a great deal to Wagner's studio. While the master accorded little place to this type of question—in *Modern Architecture* he speaks only of the influence of the environment on art—Max Fabiani, one of his collaborators, was interested in researching the different modes of expression of various peoples. Plečnik was thus freed from the temptation of ethnographic imitation, which was then part of a fashionable trend for rejuvenating national styles. The notion of the "will for art" (*Kunstwollen*), a theory that was introduced to art history at the beginning of the century by Alois Riegl, indirectly led Plečnik to ponder traditional Slovenian thought and expression. He never overtly stated his basic principles; he allowed himself to be guided by a heightened artistic sense. This led him at times to rather unexpected discoveries, though ones that in no way influenced his work (it seemed to him, for example, that there was a distinct relationship between Etruscan and Slovenian art). He remained within the Viennese architectural current, convinced that his self-discipline would lead him to the goal he had set for himself. For example, when he wrote "It seems to me I am keeping bad company and I have no greater desire than to be more and more Carniolan-Slovenian . . . to remain close to all the characteristics of my home," he was not thinking of a specific modification to his style, but of the full expression of his talents, which he believed fortified him in his style. At the same time, he was devoted to the search for a timeless art that would remain independent of trends. Nonetheless, his highly developed plastic sense and "his solid Karstian taste," which, in his own words, "is displeasing to the Viennese," distinguished him from other Austrian artists. Despite this, and even though after the earthquake in 1895 there was no lack of work in Ljubljana, Plečnik obtained no important commissions in his own country. Thwarted in his love for his homeland, he plunged even deeper into solitude. In Vienna he visited few of his fellow countrymen, especially since none wanted to follow him down the difficult road to perfection. With no hope of their being built, he continued to work on architectural projects for his native city.

Activity within the Secession

Plečnik's activity within the Secession gradually led him to settle accounts with Viennese modern art. He exhibited frequently at the Secession building; a desk presented in 1902, at the fifth exhibition, received critical praise. At this time, things began to change within the Secession. Plečnik and others were witness to the intrigues surrounding the painter Klimt at the university, to the presentation of Max Klinger's Beethoven statue, to the discovery of the Swiss Hodler, and to the opposition between its members that finally caused a rift in the movement. In 1904 he participated in the World's Fair in Saint Louis, Missouri, with a salon that earned him a gold medal and a laudatory article by H. Muthesius in the journal *Deutsche Kunst und Dekoration*. He completed this project in record time in order to help out a furniture manufacturer, even though he himself was opposed to the exhibition. "People scorn hard-earned money, and this does not lead to happiness." Despite all this, his design for the room at the World's Fair encouraged Plečnik to introduce certain stylistic innovations into the Zacherl house, which he was building at the time. His black polished furniture and great granite tabletop are experiments with dark stone, a material rarely used at the time.

Desk for the fifth
exhibition of the
Secession, Vienna,
1902

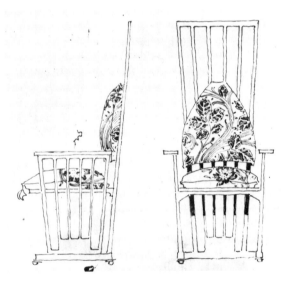

Chairs for the home
of Dr. Knauer, Vienna,
1903

The Zacherl House

The Zacherl house represents an incontestable summit in the works of Plečnik's youth (see "Portfolio" section). He obtained the commission by way of a competition while still working in his master's studio. In addition to Plečnik, Wagner also chose Max Fabiani, Franz Krauss—the latter probably upon request from the client—Otto Schönthal, and Carl Fischl. Plečnik used almost all the structural and technical particularities of Wagner's Majolika house and of Fabiani's Artaria in Kohlmarkt; on the othr hand, the plastic organizational work is all his own. One of the most obvious innovations is the increased flatness of the facade's projections. But after an initial difference with the contractors, who had been chosen by Zacherl, Plečnik withdrew, refusing to continue work, despite the exhortations of Wagner's son. It seems that only a more or less fortuitous meeting with the manufacturer caused the sensitive architect to acquiesce. As we learn from a letter to his elder brother, Plečnik returned full force to the designs in the beginning of 1903.

His friendship with the client opened new horizons for him. A rich manufacturer, Zacherl was a fervent partisan of the Catholic movement in Austria. Plečnik greatly appreciated his liberal spirit and moderation, and they agreed on certain fundamental concepts, such as the meaning and role of art and intuition. As Plečnik wrote to his brother, "He is a husband, a father, a true Catholic, and despite all this his home is not otherworldly."

The architect was particularly pleased to meet Zacherl's friends, among whom figure some influential Christian-Socialists, headed by the mayor of Vienna, Karl Leuger. From then on Plečnik remained close to the source of Catholic philosophy of the time, which encouraged him in his determination to reform sacred art.

While regularly visiting the family, Plečnik became close to Zacherl's niece. Like the Polish Irma Dutczyńska, a painter he met during his travels in Rome, she was slightly older than he and took kindly to his sensitive artistic nature. Yet the architect hesitated to marry, taking refuge in an ever greater asceticism. Marriage seemed too great an obstacle on the road to absolute art.

Plečnik soon succeeded in designing a plan for the house suitable for the irregularly shaped lot, which is bordered by streets on three sides. To satisfy the client's wish that the two floors of the store be spatially modifiable, Plečnik chose reinforced concrete load-bearing pillars for the ground floor and mezzanine; at the time this was extremely daring, as the properties of this new material were as yet only partially known. His subsequent choice of reinforced concrete for the Church of the Holy Spirit was immeasurably less risky. Moreover, the architect's

Mr. and Mrs. Zacherl in 1904

opinion was not the determining factor in the construction of the Zacherl house; the client was above all seduced by the economical aspects of François Hennebique's constructions, which the Ast company had been propagating in Austria for several years.

Plečnik attacked the staircases of the Zacherl house in an entirely new manner, giving them an elegant elliptical form, which led to a modification in the entryway. For the facade he chose the formula of rectangular grid work, which he had already used in the Melk house, adapting the windows' dimensions to suit. The treatment of the lower and upper sections represents a significant innovation. For the lower section of the mezzanine, Plečnik created a cornice to balance the eaves. The mezzanine and the top floor become transitional zones where the unified area of the building begins and ends. The new rhythm and the different proportions show that Plečnik was attempting to make a radical break from his master's influence.

The plans were practically finished when, in a chance conversation, everything was overturned. Zacherl wanted his building to resemble an old neighborhood house, with graying walls. Plečnik responded that it would be possible to do it with granite facing, an idea for which the client expressed immediate enthusiasm, despite its expense. During the Secession, the dream of a granite-style architecture was in the air: the idea was alive in Wagner's school, and Adolf Loos had written extensively on this material. Even though Wagner and Loos addressed the problematic question from an intellectual point of view, we cannot forget the symbolism and the mysticism that, at the dawn of the twentieth century, managed to seep into the school's severe framework. The monumental granite pillars in the sanctuaries of ancient Egypt had long

attracted Plečnik, who often visited the Egyptian antiquities at the art museum in Vienna. On another level, by using heavy dark colors, he was trying to oppose the white facades of the Viennese Secession. Plečnik therefore modified the rectangular forms of the post-Secession style ornamentation by use of granite facing. As it was impossible to embellish these forms without sinning against Wagnerian doctrine—according to which the ancient Egyptians had attained artistic perfection in their use of the stone by polishing it—he preferred to enliven the composition by rhythmically repeating slabs of varying sizes. Attaching the large slabs posed a particular problem. Wagner had been able to draw an aesthetic effect from this problem by metaphorically changing the construction details into *technoïde* decoration, which glorified the development of modern technology. Plečnik, however, did not believe unconditionally in the omnipotence of the machine. He opted instead for vertical strips of granite, of neutral significance, behind which he placed the heavy facing. From a moral standpoint, his solution was as justified as Wagner's use of nails, and technically it allowed for greater mobility of the slabs and the elimination of sealing joints. The strips of granite gave the building an accentuated vertical movement, which Plečnik tried to contain by using ornamentation in opposition to this verticality. He found his solution in Franz Metzner's monumental telamones, then exhibited at the Secession building. With their muscular forms these telamones balance the tensions in the facade's composition. Following the model of Viennese sidewalk borders, he had them produced in pebbledash and filled in the extra area on the top floor with an intermediary slab.

Once again, Plečnik had to change his plans at the request of the city, which required that the top floor be set back thirty degrees. This seemingly simple task led the architect, after an in-depth study, to a very convincing solution consisting of doubling the upper cornice while prolonging the proportion and outline below. The top of the building becomes a dynamic field. The telamones not only resolve the vertical and horizontal junction in the composition, they also orient the movement frontally. The facade, with its rounded angles, the treatment of which represented a departure from Wagnerian architecture, is distinguishable from the neighboring buildings only by the rhythm of its windows. But Plečnik modified it further to obtain the effect of a unified external surface, starting at the Church of Saint Steven. The drum on top of the building gives the impression of a cylinder inserted into the mass. This solution was brought to Plečnik's attention purely by chance, when he placed a box of dental powder on the model!

Part of the house's staircase was inspired by one of the most beautiful post-baroque staircases, found at the Gruber house in Ljubljana, which was threatened with destruction. To at least preserve its memory, Plečnik reproduced its elliptical form, thus transplanting an element of Slovenian culture to Vienna. Among Plečnik's finds, we must also mention the parquetry of the partitions.

At the end of November 1905, the scaffolding was removed and the building appeared in all its splendor. The critics were immediately divided into two camps. It was above all Zacherl's political opponents who attacked it, spreading rumors that the apartments were humid because of the granite facing. The avant-garde artists had an entirely different point of view and celebrated it as a new victory of the modern spirit.

The writer Peter Altenberg expressed his enthusiasm in these moving words: "It represents such a colossal force as will defeat and pulverize conformity; its heavy, muted tones will proclaim the world's new order!" Plečnik was especially pleased with the appearance of the building's exterior. When, upon his return to Prague, he built a house in Ljubljana, he chose to erect beneath the eaves, as a memory of his youth, a miniature of Metzner's telamon.

Plečnik never again produced such a convincing synthesis of the extreme avant-garde and tradition. He turned to ornamentation, as can be seen in the facade of the House for Catholic Children in Währing. The force of the granite walls found in the Zacherl house became watered down. The architect was more interested in minor commissions at the time: he decorated apartments for Zacherl and for his two married daughters, designed an altar for one of the stations in the Corpus Christi procession, and took care of the decorations for family gatherings.

The works of this period are marked by their varied content and by their ties with tradition. In 1905 Plečnik furnished one room in the apartment of Zacherl's son-in-law, Dr. Peham, in Empire style, yet filled another with astonishingly modern pieces, composed solely of geometric shapes, in which the combination of hard and soft woods is emphasized by a successful contrast between light and dark. On the whole, Plečnik paid little attention to Secession styles in matters of furnishings. He studied mostly English models, completing the elegance of his compositions with bold details. An accomplished woodworker, he remained resolutely faithful to classical methods and showed no particular interest in curved wood.

The successful exhibition of sacred art sponsored by the Secession in 1905 also resulted from the ties between the architect and the manufacturer Zacherl. After Klimt's departure, a large group of Plečnik's friends remained in the movement. He got along particularly well with the new president, the painter and sculptor Ferdinand Andri. That the exhibition united the works of monks from the German monastery of Beuron with those of formerly denounced avant-garde artists struck Plečnik as somewhat miraculous. In religious circles, the monks' art represented hope for the future, and Plečnik believed in their mission, despite their evident eclecticism and the unevenness of their work. Even while he tried to rid modern art of any false sentimentality, he was at times unexpectedly moved by pious subjects of paintings and sculpture. Later on, for example, he placed a realistic statue of Christ the Savior in the crypt of his Church of the Holy Spirit in Vienna, which even today intrigues the visitor by its violent contrast with the resolutely modern character of the architecture. In his very fundamental faith, Plečnik was undoubtedly close to the Catalan Antonio Gaudì.

Plečnik profoundly hated the idea of "art for art's sake." For him, art must have a clear objective, which only a morally irreproachable creator could ensure. Although not very familiar with Ruskin's philosophy, he readily approved of some of his ideas and believed that the moral life of previous generations had conditioned the artistic talent of the generations that followed.

With a few exceptions, the period following the completion of the Zacherl house was a rather sterile one for the architect. In 1909 he collaborated on the construction of the Karl-Borromaüs fountain to commemorate the sixtieth birthday of Vienna's mayor, Karl Leuger; his friend Josef Engelhardt had begun work on the fountain in the third administrative district. But the project dragged on and on, and Plečnik gradually lost all interest in its design, which was still deeply influenced by the Secession. The fountain is not a bad piece of work on the whole, especially in its spatial organization. Plečnik added depth to the square, which is squeezed between four streets; a low elliptical-shaped wall protects it from the surrounding commotion. Some of the elements, which he modeled himself in his friend Engelhardt's studio, also turned out quite well, revealing his talent as a sculptor.

Karl-Borromaüs fountain. Plečnik and Joseph Engelhart in the sculptor's workshop in Vienna in 1908.

As he did for the staircase of the Zacherl house, Plečnik once again brought to Vienna an element from the artistic tradition of his native land. He found inspiration this time in the Venetian Francesco Robba's baroque fountain, situated in front of the Ljubljana City Hall; he also resolved certain problems in composition that were causing Engelhardt great difficulties.

Plečnik welcomed the decline of the Secession, for now he could freely turn to antiquity. Thus, around 1909 he placed twisted baroque columns on the facade of the Zacherl family home in Döbling, a suburb of Vienna. Yet Plečnik's evolution cannot be reduced to a simple return to the past. While we might have expected him to turn his back on the avant-garde and follow the well-trodden path of eclecticism, he produced plans for a facade in reinforced concrete for the Stollwerk chocolate factory that was refused by the authorities for "aesthetic reasons." It consisted of a simple architectural composition, adapted to the technology of new materials. This oscillation between two extremes, which also characterizes the Church of the Holy Spirit in Vienna, was not a mark of instability but an intentional search for diverse possibilities of expression, inspired by an intense desire to create.

Stollwerk factory, Vienna, design for facade, 1910

Zacherl house, Döbling, plan of facade, 1909

The Church of the Holy Spirit

The Church of the Holy Spirit in Ottakring, the fruit of ten years of painstaking research and experimentation, is a synthesis of the work of Plečnik's youth (see "Portfolio" section). He began by attempting to improve on Wagnerian schemes, then gradually became committed to the idea of a church that would be more functional—from a liturgical standpoint—and would better correspond to his desire to "democratize" the church. Although his return to the models of the first Christians resembles the premises of Beuron, Plečnik was also attempting to reform the religious architecture of his time in accordance with Wagner's principles. On the whole, he was ready to subordinate the building's form to its function. At a time when Wagner was creating a prototype for the work of total modern art with his Steinhof Church, Plečnik's church was barely more than a meeting place for Christian Socialism amid the proletariat of one of Vienna's poorest suburbs. Plečnik was shocked that one of the most representative sacred works of the period was entrusted to Wagner, who publicly aspired to a "style without confession"; in the Czech journal *Styl,* he vigorously attacked the arbitrary and ineffectual manner in which Wagner approached the construction of churches, ending an enumeration of various technical and liturgical inadequacies with this cry: "Better no art than this art!"

When the Society of Léon opened a competition in 1902, Plečnik shifted the focus of his thought from fantastic facades to the study of a rational layout for a church. His study especially confirmed him in his choice of a traditional longitudinal nave between the altar and the portal. Only in the distribution of the chapels did he allow himself greater freedom. With particular love, he even designed a chapel dedicated to the Sacred Heart near the altar, in memory of his mother.

Of all his master's lessons, Plečnik respected above all that of the visibility of the main altar. But in Prague, while contemplating the lateral nave of a church, it occurred to him that the service could also be held in more recessed areas. His first innovation was an "altar wall" for the Secession's exhibition of sacred art. The following year he developed plans for a church in Vienna, which was never built.

Plečnik produced the first sketches for Ottakring's new church in 1908, upon the request of Father Franz Unterhofer. He did not expect much from this offer, for until then all commissions of this type, including the expansion of the Franciscan church in Trsat-above-the-Rijeka, had slipped through his fingers. He did not begin to work on it until the following autumn, and then only to please Unterhofer. Plečnik modified his plans constantly to comply with Unterhofer's changing demands, repeatedly reducing and monumentalizing them, with no concern for the eventual cost. In April of 1910 Wagner's 1906–7 variation on a provisional church inspired him to find an expressive solution. He added windows on both sides of a sloping roof, beneath which, on the interior, he placed the Stations of the Cross. When, shortly afterward, those commissioning the church requested a large room beneath it, he returned to work. By resolving questions of form, he created a simple interior space and the most practical liaison possible between this room, the crypt, and the nave. The priest's residence was to be under the same roof, in an extension behind the choir.

We do not know what brought about this optimistic extension in the plans, which in effect created a full-fledged religious center with a monumental presbytery and lodgings instead of the simple church originally intended. The patronage of the Duchess of Hohenberg, the wife of the heir-apparent to the throne, who wanted to dedicate this church to the Holy Spirit, probably encouraged the members of the council. Plečnik seized the opportunity, sparing neither materials nor ornamentation. He indefatigably altered the church's exterior without taking into account that it would have to be built economically—in concrete—without two of the planned neighboring buildings and without the bell tower. As construction was about to begin, in autumn of 1910, Plečnik tried to abandon the project. He informed his brother Andrej:

Along with this letter, I will be posting another to Unterhofer to turn down the church. Let them begin in the spring! They can finish it according to my plans, but let them entrust the construction to someone more competent. The hunt for money is now beginning. All this is so foreign to me, so unpleasant that I feel ill in my body and soul.

The real disaster occurred when those commissioning the church requested a subvention from the Ministry of Culture. Plečnik's plans were passed through the wheels of government, and the Ministry of Public Works refused them. At this point, Wagner, who never forgot his student, began a suit to defend Plečnik's church, using as his base the Austrian Association of Engineers and Architects. At the beginning of 1911 François-Ferdinand declared outright that the church was "a combination Russian bath, stable, and sanctuary of Venus" and demanded that the architect transform his church into a basilica with columns. Plečnik firmly rejected this outrageous request, thus permanently

angering the prince. Following this incident, Plečnik became an outcast; the church was saved only because the contract with the construction company had already been signed. Like everyone else, the court's prelate, Swoboda, turned his back on Plečnik, thus depriving him of all hope to one day build another church in Austria. The state's subvention proved to be inadequate and new patrons had to be found, which led to a reduction in the plans and unwarranted interference in the architect's work.

Plečnik's love for early Christian architecture strongly influenced the project. Although on paper the church is almost a square, the lateral aisles give it the feel of a basilica. To render the altar more visible, the architect rejected the use of intermediary pillars and chose a construction method that until then had mostly been used for bridges. After many attempts to impose the use of a wooden ceiling, in the end he had to abandon this idea, faced with the fire department's stern recommendations. The crypt is all the more significant from a plastic perspective, as Plečnik was able to give the design of its columns, borrowed from the basement of a bank designed by Wagner, entirely new dimensions. They constitute one of the first examples of cubism in architecture, as well as the first appearance of mushroom vaulting (*pilzdecke*), even though they still support traditional beams.

Within the context of the development of architecture, we must insist on Plečnik's revolutionary effort to pave the way for monumental architecture in reinforced concrete. He especially studied its textural qualities, using either smooth or bumpy surfaces, and occasionally fought against concrete's gloomy gray tones by adding crushed brick. It is not surprising that on a formal level Plečnik frequently sought inspiration in antiquity, as seen in his proto-Doric columns, chosen because they were naturally adapted to coffers. For the church's facade, he drew away from Wagnerian decoration and began experimenting with the extreme stylization of historical forms made possible by new technology. The carefully balanced facade is inspired by the neoclassical current found at the time in the works of other Viennese architects. The two apertures above the tympanum, reminiscent of a belltower in Karst, were once again architectonic characteristics of Plečnik's native country.

Plečnik's church holds a special place in the sacred architecture of this period. It is comparable to an almost contemporaneous church by another student of Wagner's, Istvan Benkó, in Mul'a, a village on the Hungaro-Slovakian border. Built in reinforced concrete, the church is marked by an evident desire to introduce national expression into architecture. Benkó had spent some time in Paris working for François Hennebique and was enthusiastic about the technical possibilities of the new material. This is why he was able to realize Wagner's idea for constructing a sacred place following the most economical formula. Thus within the framework of the former monarchy, Plečnik and Benkó, each in his own way, were able to realize two aspects of Wagner's architecture: the first, by use of proportions adapted to the materials, and the second by continuing the study and development of Wagnerian projects.

The Church of the Holy Spirit is a milestone in modern sacred architecture. Here for the first time concrete was used as something other than an inexpensive substitute to produce technically complex historical elements such as cupolas and vaults. The idea would later be perfected in the architecture of Auguste Perret.

Church of the Holy Spirit, Vienna, design for the crypt, 1910

The Prague Period

Pedagogical Activities

With the help of his friend Kotěra, Plečnik was appointed to a teaching position at the Prague School of Applied Arts in February 1911, where he received a regular salary and, for the first time since completing his studies, enjoyed university vacations. He also escaped the rising German nationalism then taking place in Vienna and could devote himself to the study of Slavic art. Yet upon his arrival in Prague, he became intrigued by the reigning liberal climate.

Plečnik in 1912

Until the beginning of World War I, Plečnik returned frequently to Vienna, where Unterhofer was working hard and having great difficulty finishing the Church of the Holy Spirit. Having put so much of his ideals and hopes into this church, Plečnik remained faithful to it until the end. Without remuneration he drew plans for the modification of the facade during construction and took charge of the interior decoration. He was a regular visitor to the Zacherl home in Döbling, where the manufacturer always offered him some commission, such as designs for the annex of the house or the family altar in the neighboring Carmelite church. Despite the many difficulties he encountered, Vienna remained a part of his homeland, whereas he was unfamiliar with Prague and the Czechs. Given his rather inflexible nature, he continued to speak German long after his arrival in Prague. He spent his days behind the walls of the school and his nights reading, while hoping to return to Vienna to try his luck once again.

After a year of teaching in Prague, Plečnik was offered a chair at the Academy of Prussia, a tempting position that he nonetheless refused. Once again he had to make an important decision. Despite his enthusiasm for the pan-Slavic ideal, shortly afterward he refused an offer by the Dalmatian sculptor Ivan Mestrović and the art critic Strajnić to organize a School of Applied Arts in Belgrade.

Wagner's Retirement

Plečnik was far more concerned with what was going on during the same period regarding a successor to Wagner at the Academy of Fine Arts in Vienna. His disappointment in this affair was proportionate to the emotion aroused in him at the idea of an eventual return to Vienna. Wagner's retirement was on the agenda as early as the academic year 1911–12. The old professor had prepared a small exhibition of the works of his best students, that is, of potential candidates to replace him. The committee of professors unanimously chose Plečnik. No one dreamed that Prince François-Ferdinand had entirely different plans for the school upon Wagner's retirement, as it had been bothering him for some time. The ministry delayed Wagner's departure for one year. The next year, the same thing happened, with Wagner's students supporting Plečnik's candidacy ever more vehemently. The minister maintained his position, and by the third selection Plečnik's name appeared next to that of Léopold Bauer, for whom the prince opted. The choice of Bauer the "renegade," as Wagner called him, provoked some turmoil among the students, leading to the questioning of the minister in Parliament. Meanwhile, though his name filled the newspaper columns, Plečnik had already buried the idea of a return to Vienna.

In Prague he replaced Kotěra, and, in the words of Paval Janák, reoriented the school's revolutionary modernity toward "a mature modern classicism." He encountered difficulties in his teaching, as the majority of his students lacked the sophistication necessary to understand him. For the most part, Plečnik returned to the pedagogical practices of Wagner's school. He raised his students' cultural level by encouraging them to participate in exhibitions and by organizing excursions; he increased their willingness to innovate by exposing them to new works. In his words:

The important thing is not who is guiding the student. A master has but one obligation: to help his student to learn, to see and to discover that one must continue to be optimistic in order to inspire confidence. The rest is unimportant. Life grabs each man in its arms of steel and pierces him with thorns . . . If I served as a guide, I did so naively, without the slightest maxim, and I will continue to do so as long as it is God's will.

Candlestick for the altar of the Zacherl family chapel

Plečnik's formula was therefore no different from that of Wagner, who constantly recommended that his students go into life with their eyes open. The former merely added a moral obligation, "Look inside as well, that is, into your soul, and be careful not to neglect it!"

In 1914 Plečnik, along with Kotěra, Gočár, and Kamil Hilbert, was among the founders of Společnost Architektů, an association of architects opposed to the official academicism of Czech architecture. Plečnik was, if not the central personality around whom the young generation gathered, at least someone of whom they all expected a great deal. Some of his most sensitive students managed to adopt a degree of cubism, either by referring to solutions such as the plans for the Stollwerk factory or by immediately accepting the new forms proposed by the protagonists of the movement. The works produced at the school, published at the end of 1912 in the Společnost Architektů journal *Styl,* are an interesting mixture of the classical (in the style of Plečnik), the patriotic (focusing on the nationalist theme), and of cubism (representing the avant-garde). Cubism continued to play a decisive role in the drawings of Plečnik's students, but it was reduced to the level of simple decoration. Indeed, Plečnik never allowed form to invade or disturb structure, just as he scrupulously assured that an exaggerated taste for popular art did not lead to mere copying.

Plečnik received no important commissions during his stay in Prague, creating only one funerary monument for a village cemetery in Křivoklát. During World War I, in addition to his architecture classes, he taught industrial design to students in the metalworking section. Thus after many years, he once again had occasion to involve himself in the craft of the gold- and silversmith. He was particularly interested in chalices and other liturgical objects, which he created for his brother Andrej. In 1913, as part of a competition for a monument dedicated to the Hussites' hero, Jan Žižka, Plečnik suggested a statue before a giant spherical shell in concrete, embellished by a chalice in an elegant, and, once again, symbolic form. Around this time, his study of chalices also gave rise to a collection of beautiful chandeliers destined for the Zacherl family altar in Vienna (see "Portfolio" section).

During the war years, which were harshly felt in Prague, Plečnik reoriented himself toward the decorative arts, as he could expect no important commissions from Czechoslovakia or from his own country, where no one even remembered him.

Nostalgia for Home

Plečnik returned to his country of birth more and more frequently, thus strengthening ties with his family. He traveled a great deal with Andrej, particularly throughout the Karst region, and for the first time became truly acquainted with the art of his country. He grew concerned that the lack of sensitivity of foreign architects was causing Ljubljana to lose its "character," acquired over the centuries from its proximity to Italy, and began reflecting on the capital's city planning problems. The years without commissions were also a period of maturation for Plečnik, giving way to an intense desire to return permanently to Slovenia.

The end of the war brought about fundamental changes at the School of Applied Arts in Prague. Designs for monuments and pavilions gave way to more important commissions. *Stavitel* and *Styl,* two influential trade journals that supported Plečnik, show his students playing an incontestable role in the agitated postwar period. The increase in construction also brought Plečnik into the public eye, manifested by his nomination to many juries. He did not work on any projects at this time, so as "not to take bread from the mouths of his colleagues in Prague," as he put it. His mind was already in Ljubljana, which is why he accepted only small commissions of a religious nature for Slovenia.

The atmosphere at the Prague School was soon disturbed by debates about recognition of the professional titles it granted, debates directed especially against Kotěra's and Plečnik's first students. It was believed for some time that the doctoral level of studies could become a joint program with the Academy of Fine Arts in Prague. Gočár and Janák, who began acting as the unauthorized representatives of Czech architecture, became unpleasantly noisy. It seems that these events caused Plečnik to withdraw and move closer to the newly founded University of Ljubljana. Yet it was a difficult step to take, especially since the Czechs, once again by way of Kotěra, were offering him the chair of the architecture department at the Academy of Fine Arts in Prague. In response to the exhortations of his friends, and to numerous letters from the vice-chancellor, he stated, but in a confused manner, his sole desire to return to his native country.

Indecision caused Plečnik to avoid responding to an invitation from Ljubljana, even though he had already expressed his desire to return home to Ivan Vurnik, director of the architecture department. As he was unknown in his country, the committee of professors made him a serious offer only after Max Fabiani refused the position. They were also encouraged by the offer from the Academy in Prague, news of which had reached Ljubljana. Before his return to Slovenia, Plečnik's sole project in the country had been the plans for a modest building to house the Technical School of Ljubljana. As his decision was as yet unclear, at the end of 1920 he was invited to Zagreb, where the monograph by Strajnić had just made him famous.

Prague Castle

A new offer at the last minute caused him to change his mind and delay his departure. Shortly after his election, Tomáš G. Masaryk, president of the Czech republic, shrewdly addressed the problems of urban development in the capital and the restoration of Prague Castle, whose rich historical tradition was to make it the national center of the young republic. A competition was opened in 1920 for the Rajská Zahrada Garden (Garden of Paradise). Plečnik was first nominated to sit on the jury and then chosen for his proposal in May of the same year. He met Masaryk in mid-November while preparing the plans; shortly afterward the latter, following the suggestions of the Mánes group, promoted Plečnik to the rank of castle architect.

There was something extraordinary about the meeting of this inner-directed artist and the philosopher and famous politician, whose outlook differed in many ways. Masaryk sought an inspired creator whose architecture could express the very values on which the Czech state had been based, intending, among other projects, to personally finance a monument to those who had died for freedom. Plečnik, sensitive enough to understand his ideas, suggested an obelisk that would be visible from afar, lit by a perpetual flame honoring the fallen soldiers. This obelisk, the foundations for which were already being laid in the early 1920s, remained one of the central themes in the reorganization of the castle. Plečnik constantly reworked his project, but after a mishap in the transportation of the granite monolith, he lacked the courage to complete it. Realizing the creative force he had unleashed in the architect, Masaryk patiently bore these ups and downs.

Initially, no one knew how to satisfy the president; Masaryk wanted the castle's restoration to be as simple as possible, while improving it aesthetically and symbolizing ideas of national independence and democracy. "The nation regards the castle as a national monument; hence we must transform a castle intended for the monarchy into a democratic castle," Masaryk noted in his 1925 declaration. It is clear why only partial solutions had been envisaged earlier, ones that often bore an eminently conservative stamp.

The affinities between the architect and Alice, the president's daughter, gradually led to a more global approach to the treatment of the castle. Like her father, Alice believed in Plečnik's mission. Cultured, entirely devoted to the idea of a nation, she carried out the difficult task entrusted to her, which often got her caught between Plečnik, the sensitive artist; Karel Fiala, the pragmatic engineer; and various ministers trying to gain political benefit from the castle project. At first Alice was skeptical, fearing that Plečnik would "lose sight of Czech history" in the course of the renovation, but as their relationship developed into platonic love, she faithfully supported his ideas.

Plečnik found himself caught in the crossfire from the Czech public, which often saw him as an unwelcome foreigner. Masaryk and his daughter wanted the castle to develop into a kind of pan-national acropolis, while introducing a new Slavic style in architecture. Masaryk, who was educated in traditional European philosophy, supported Plečnik's classical roots, while Alice's affinities were with the small-town pastoral environment of sub-Carpathian Russia. She remained convinced that the integrity of the Slovakian soul would save the Czechs from materialism, an opinion shared by Plečnik. With

his students from Ljubljana, where he began teaching in 1921–22, he traversed a large part of Slovakia on foot, discovering the authentic values of the people. He felt especially close to the Slovaks because of their destiny as a "non-historical nation," which was also that of the Slovenians.

Plečnik skillfully navigated the dangers of classicism and the folkloric, carefully avoiding elements that could weaken the expressive force of his work. With nearly unlimited means at his disposal, he wanted to produce important monolithic pieces, in which he saw a kind of equivalence with antiquity. Yet despite the most modern technical means, the realization of his ideas carried with it many risks. Much of his behavior can be understood as a way to measure himself against the great creators of the past.

None of Plečnik's creations can compare in importance and breadth to the restoration of Prague Castle (see "Portfolio" section). The architect went to work with astonishing enthusiasm and returned to Prague each year during school vacations until 1935. He began work in the gardens and in the western part of the castle. Vestiges of the tiers of a former amphitheater, discovered on the edge of the Garden of Paradise, gave Plečnik the idea for a large flight of stairs, in the middle of which would be erected the memorial obelisk. Below, he placed a basin carved from a single block of granite on a large carpet of grass. After many sketches inspired by conventional fountains, he returned to the idea of a large block of natural material in a simple form that would give off the same aura of monumentality as the smooth walls of the Zacherl house. The obelisk, which was to be crowned by the Czech lion executed by the

Prague Castle, bird's-eye view of the three courtyards and the gardens

sculptor Štursa, required far greater efforts: in 1923, extraction began of a block of granite almost nineteen meters long, which was to be sculpted at the castle. The idea received much attention, not only from the public at large, lovers of sensationalism, but also from specialists. Masaryk entrusted the transport of the monolith to the Škoda factories and to the army. When a piece of the future monument cracked, Plečnik took it badly, far worse than did Masaryk, who was paying for the stone. The enormous block remained at the castle for four years before Plečnik returned to work on it and installed it in the third courtyard, now sculpted in a simpler fashion. Neither the president nor his daughter could persuade him to complete his initial idea.

Extraction of a granite
block for the obelisk,
c. 1923

Transporting the
obelisk

**Preparation of the
granite basin for the
Garden of Paradise,
c. 1923**

**Transporting the
basin**

**Installation of the
basin**

The Garden of Paradise was followed by the narrow and incredibly long Garden on the Ramparts. During 1923 and 1924, Plečnik rid it of its later additions and gave it greater architectonic interest by creating a belvedere under the Theresa wing of the castle, an oval-shaped horizontal beam in granite in front of the Obelisk of Slovat, the Fountain of Samson, an aviary, a staircase leading to the alpine arboretum beneath the ramparts, a pergola with a granite table, and an obelisk on a "Moravian bastion." The partial reduction and demolition of the garden wall, which was not particularly old, aroused heated debates. Plečnik opened up new vistas to the city, including the bell towers and cupolas of the churches of Prague. Beneath the winter garden, which has since been modified, he installed a great panoramic terrace, and for reasons of perspective placed an elegant stone pyramid nearby. A few years later and not far away, he installed a slightly smaller panoramic pavilion.

**Prague Castle, Garden
on the Ramparts,
1923–24**

Prague Castle, Garden on the Ramparts

Prague Castle, Garden on the Ramparts, panoramic terrace

Prague Castle, Garden of the Bastion

In the second half of the twenties, while creating the tiled pavement for the third courtyard, he restored the Garden "na Baště" (of the Bastion). He divided the undifferentiated architectonic space into two parts: a courtyard, which he paved and connected to the two other courtyards with new passageways, and a garden on a slightly higher level. In the center he installed a circular stairway in the style of Bramante, an idea he often returned to later. Using cypress trees, he clearly delineated the passageway running from the pavement to a sandy area and ending in a grassy garden, left in its original state, beneath the entrance to the Spanish room. To the north he effectively concluded the overlapping of levels and of passageways with a staircase leading to the Jeleni Přikop (Deer Moat) and with a ramp toward Prašný Bridge (Powder Bridge). With these extensions, he opened the castle on all sides, ridding it as much as possible of its fortress style. In front of the Spanish room, on the foundations of the former watchtower and in

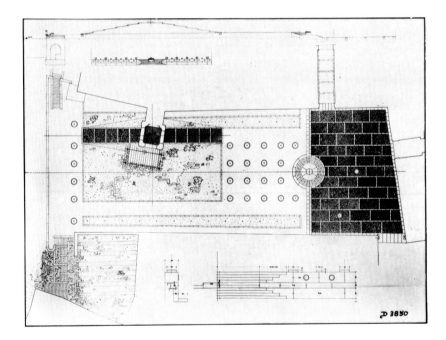

Prague Castle, plan for the Garden of the Bastion, 1927

defiance of the principles dictating the disposition of historical monuments, he placed a very Mediterranean style pergola. Although Masaryk wanted Plečnik to work on other gardens to the north of the castle, the architect was content to plant a vineyard at the top of the Deer Moat in the late twenties. He created a panoramic terrace surrounding the great lime tree, accessed directly by a tiered passageway.

In designing the pavement for the first courtyard, Plečnik used darker stones to indicate a new direction, thereby avoiding Mathias gate, a symbol of Hapsburg domination. In order to emphasize the president's wish to eliminate any hint of the Austrian reign, he envisioned sealing off the principal door with glass. He modified the function of the first courtyard by creating two new openings in the main wing: one to the north, before the Spanish room, used for official functions. For the other, which gave access to Masaryk's apartments, he utilized a path, abandoned since the seventeenth century, running along the southern side of the courtyard. In the late twenties he demolished a large part of the internal structure of the main wing—which

lacked homogeneity—to the north of the Mathias gate, and, in a great creative thrust, designed a four-story entryway into the Spanish room. This room, later to be called the Plečnik room, can be seen as the peristyle leading to the new Czech acropolis. We find this idea in other architectural ensembles of deliberately symbolic conception, such as the University Library in Ljubljana or the entrance to the "City of the Dead" in Žale. With discerning taste, Plečnik designed ceilings adorned with copper plating atop Ionic columns. Following the model of the cedar poles at San Marco square in Venice, he placed two masts twenty-five meters high, in Moravian pine, near the Mathias gate. Despite subsequent alterations, it is practically impossible today to distinguish the attempts made by Plečnik to "democratize" the first courtyard, for in many places the pre-1920 state has been restored.

One of his most daring interventions in Prague was the paving of the third courtyard. Recently completed archaeological digs furnished a mass of new information about the oldest buildings—situated between the Cathedral of Saint

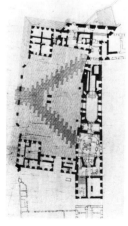

Prague Castle, plan of the paving of the first courtyard, 1922

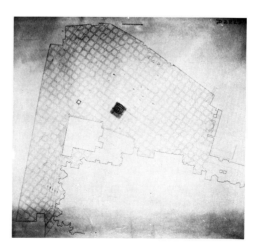

Prague Castle, plan of the paving of the third courtyard, 1928

**Prague Castle, Plečnik
Room, 1926–28**

Guy and the southern wing of the castle—which Plečnik had to respect. What is more, the slight southern incline of this courtyard made a unified conception difficult. Plečnik opted for the most radical solution. He leveled the courtyard so that a part of the cathedral's foundations appeared above ground on the northern side, while to the southeast a part of the former royal palace was swallowed up by a new granite slab. A special ramp had to be constructed to provide access. He also had to display the archaeological discoveries, which dated from the first Czech state and were of national interest. To protect them, he built a concrete roof the length of the cathedral; to the south, however, he conserved them in basements recently constructed beneath the courtyard.

It is probably in the stairway leading from the southeast angle of the courtyard to the Garden on the Ramparts that national symbolism was most developed. Its axis connects the golden door of the cathedral to the former seat of the Czech kings of Vyšehrad. In the stairway, four oxen support a canopy. The allusion to the myth of the Czech Queen Libuša and her peasant fiancé, Přmysl, seems to be founded on iconography. From a formal perspective, the copper placed between two wooden beams is reminiscent of cloth and expresses, in Semper style, the idea of the independence of form and material. Of all the different types of stairways, Plečnik finally chose one very close to that found in the Chamber of Commerce, Crafts, and Industry in Ljubljana. In the classical association of folklore with antiquity, its resemblance to a staircase of the royal palace in Knossos was probably no accident, and Alice Masaryk had often stated that Czechoslovakia was the Greece of the Slavic world. Plečnik finished his work on the castle with the former Convent of Noble Ladies, to the east of what is known as the Chancellery of Bohemia.

In September 1921 it was decided that Prague Castle would house only the apartments of the president of the republic. The greatly neglected wing situated above the Garden of Paradise therefore had to be radically reorganized, both technically and aesthetically. Upon the founding of the state, Jan Kotěra had designed the first projects for reorganization, but Masaryk and his daughter were not entirely satisfied with these plans and entrusted the task to Plečnik. Masaryk's library was to be central to the new apartment; Alice wanted this library to become a kind of national sanctuary. While the first-floor reception rooms conserved their original baroque pieces, completed by recent acquisitions of period furnishings, the second floor had to be entirely redesigned. Plečnik began by constructing a nearly circular staircase, then moved on to an elevator in the narrow passage between the chapel and the main wing, and finally widened the stairway in the Garden of Paradise.

In order to unite the entire series of rooms joined by a corridor and create a spacious, bright central area in the apartment, Plečnik created an impluvium at the intersection of the southern and main wings. He opened it up on four sides with large arches and installed a granite fountain in the form of a shallow basin. He took full advantage of the castle's irregular spaces. While in the city Czech architects were practicing a cubism glazed with national romanticism—later called rondo-cubism—and were beginning to discover the expressionistic qualities of modern Dutch architecture, at the castle time stood still. Plečnik's renovation was done as an uncompromising search for the absolute in art.

Prague Castle, room
in the White Tower,
1923

Prague Castle, chair
for Alice Masaryk's
salon, 1925

Prague Castle,
President Masaryk's
apartments, the
impluvium, 1924

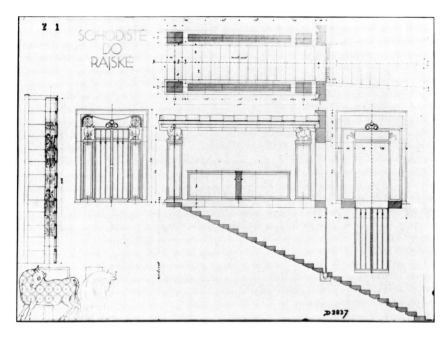

Prague Castle, plan of the canopy over the stairs leading to the Garden of Paradise, 1925

Prague Castle, canopy over the stairs leading to the Garden of Paradise, 1930

In the mid-twenties, Plečnik attended to the Ladies' Salon, still called the Embroidering Room. As Alice wanted this room to be infused with a Slovakian atmosphere, he used dark wood, decorated with popular embroideries— chosen for their quality—as well as ceramics.

The extreme delicacy of his furnishings allowed him to produce a convincing synthesis between art with a capital A and national art. In the former White Tower (Bílá Věž), around which a partition wing had been constructed, Plečnik envisaged, at the same time as the impluvium, an armory room. In the center he placed a table in solid teak, intended for the signing of official documents, underneath which he had inscribed on a marble plaque: "Submit individual concerns to the collective concern," a thought that Masaryk had taken from an old quote by Kutná Hora. For all these pieces, Plečnik collaborated with the best craftsmen, often with some of his students who had remained faithful to the applied arts.

During the summer of 1921, while still working on the castle, Plečnik began renovation of the presidential residence in Lany. Here it was more a matter of rearranging the existing furnishings than of inventing new ones. Among the works that bond the residence to the village, the Monument to the Victims of the First World War (1926) at the entrance to the park is noteworthy. Against a circular pillar, he boldly placed a roughly carved, extraordinarily long and slender piece of granite, which he secured with four steel cables. On it he intended to have this symbolic inscription engraved: "I am as fragile as freedom." The monolith at Lany represents the summit of Plečnik's research on static properties; it was inspired by the elegant Monument to the Dead at Prague Castle. Plečnik intended to crown his Ionic capital with the statue of an eagle.

When Jan Kotěra died in 1923, his students nominated Plečnik to replace him at the Prague Academy. Masaryk and his daughter strongly encouraged Plečnik to accept the position, which would allow him to more easily accomplish his pan-Slavic mission and thus, indirectly, to be useful to his country. Plečnik, who was constantly hesitating between Ljubljana and Prague, refused the chair in Prague. Masaryk tried in vain to increase the architect's attachment to Prague. In 1926 he named him a member of the Work Academy; and by giving him the title of castle architect, he made the university professor's role official for the duration of work on the castle.

Nine years later, Masaryk abdicated. Plečnik left the castle with him, well aware that his Prague odyssey was coming to an end. Even though the new government, out of respect for the first

president of the republic, manifested its intention to complete the restoration of the castle's grounds, the political climate had changed to such a degree that it was no longer possible. Thus, in addition to the monolith and its perpetual flame, another essential idea for the castle's renovation was left undone: the creation of an organic link to the city. For nearly fifteen years Plečnik had energetically addressed the question of the plateau of Letná, to the east of the castle, and of the monumental access to the national Czech acropolis. In February of 1920 Masaryk created a special national planning commission, charged with overseeing Prague's long-term development. But as the Czech president had not included the castle in its jurisdiction, reserving it for Plečnik, frequent differences arose between the commission and the Slovenian architect. Until 1926 all projects were hampered by the uncertainty surrounding a future railway line.

With the fall of the Austro-Hungarian empire, both Plečnik and Alice had experienced national liberation as the realization of Queen Libuša's prophetic vision: "I see a city whose glory will reach the stars." For this reason they sought to emphasize the historical elements that would strike a chord within the Czech collective conscience. Two essential ideas ran throughout Plečnik's plans: one was a direct link with the old city of Prague (a link between Venceslas Square and the Square of the Old City with the castle); the other, a wide Via Regia on the castle's hillside. While in 1920 Plečnik proposed access to the castle by the Mala Strana, two years later he changed his mind, choosing the Klarov district and thus abandoning the expensive construction of a bridge over the Vltava, which had been part of the first project. The idea of a monumental curve went back to Plečnik's student days, when, under Wagner's influence, he had contemplated what he called the city's crown. This was to be a great sanctuary or a national monument, at which one would arrive by way of a wide road, winding among something like the Stations of the Cross, or a series of statues of famous men. He only arrived at a definitive solution for Prague in 1928, after being pressured by the decision of the national planning commission that, in the meantime, had laid the groundwork for the city's subsequent development. He resolved the delicate city planning question with a curve in Jelení Příkop that, without much demolition, made possible the passage to the heights of the castle's hill.

An avenue approximately eighteen meters wide was to lead to the north of the castle, to a lane forty-five meters wide. But the trajectory of the lane and the organization of Letná, which was connected to it, had been envisaged much too ideally for agreement to be reached, given the very pragmatic guidelines of the planning commission. Plečnik and Alice Masaryk had in fact planned to erect propylaea on Letná (on the prolongation of the new Marianska Lane) before each ministry, the parliament, and a monumental church, while another avenue, to the west of the castle, symbolically arrived before the immense palace of Masaryk's Work Academy, a building reminiscent of the Pantheon. For Letná's plateau, several public competitions had been announced, the results of which differed from Plečnik's ideas in that they treated it as an autonomous urban project, whereas Plečnik linked it to a project for the whole of the castle. He still intended to place several other important national constructions the length of the lane: a theater, ramparts, a military cemetery, and so on. None of these ideas were realized, not even Masaryk's great library, work on which had never been started, though the plans were well advanced.

Return to Ljubljana

When he returned to his native country at the age of fifty, Plečnik was on the threshold of his most fertile period. He fled the agitation of the city, choosing to live in a single-story house situated behind the parish church of Trnovo, with a garden that extended into the surrounding fields. He dreamed of a house that would reunite his entire family and began by building a round annex; but only Janez, his youngest brother, came to stay with him for a short while. Believing in his destiny as the spiritual representative of a small nation, he devoted all his energy to realizing the dreams of his youth, but was often thwarted by middle-class attitudes and the egoism of certain town leaders. His enthusiasm was also checked by the Serbian politics of centralization, which threatened the existence of the newly created Slovenian Technical School. He himself became somewhat disenchanted, for while in Prague he had a privileged position, in Ljubljana he found almost no material means for the realization of his plans.

The study of local architecture drew him closer to the baroque tradition. He was particularly attracted to the early eighteenth century, a period when the artistic influence of Venice was key to central Slovenia; and this, as well as the Byzantine architecture of Yugoslavia, were sources of inspiration.

Continuing his pedagogical activities, he involved his students in greater participation by creating a center for architecture students: a circle that sought to popularize architecture, organize educational voyages, and edit scholarly publications. His charisma was such that his students imitated everything about him, including his handwriting and style of dress. Many later found themselves struggling with doubt, seeking their own style between the art of Pleč-nik and functionalism. However, this especially concerned the first generation of students and less their successors, who were busy doing practical work for their master's projects.

Le Corbusier's Influence on Ljubljana

In the mid-twenties, the renown of French and German architects (Le Corbusier, Perret) reached Ljubljana, disturbing the idyllic cohesion of Plečnik's school. Plečnik used a German expression to characterize the work of Le Corbusier: *"Es ist auch eine Idee aber keine von Gott kommende"* ("It's an idea, but it isn't inspired by God"). Plečnik saw Le Corbusier's work as an outgrowth of Swiss Protestantism, which he believed could give rise to a social and hygienic architecture but was incapable of going beyond pure utilitarianism. The journey to the World Architectural Exhibition of Paris in 1925 (which Plečnik purposely avoided) made a strong impression on his more sensitive students, for they felt that modern architecture was following paths different from those studied at the Technical School in Ljubljana. Many of them later frequented Le Corbusier's studio; the great French architect loved to receive Plečnik's students because of the discipline of their drawings, and he respectfully called the aged Slovenian artist "the first-rate draftsman with the trembling hand."

Sacred Architecture

In Ljubljana Plečnik developed a relationship with the parish, and especially with Father Franc Tomc, a Jesuit, who supported his efforts at reform. But at first the church did not have much work for the artist, whose credo was "Sacred architecture has been and will remain the model for profane architecture." His dream of restoring the place of pilgrimage of Sveta Gora, near Gorizia, destroyed during the First World War, was never attained. In Ljubljana he

had to begin with small projects. The Jesuits offered him only the enlargement of their monastery and the restoration of their historical church. His attempt to enlarge the Church of Saint Madeleine in Maribor, which he delegated to his assistant France Tomažič due to his commitments at Prague Castle, came to an unfortunate end.

Saint Francis Church, Šiška

While the archdiocese of Ljubljana continued to be wary of Plečnik, the Franciscans called on him for the construction of a church, but quickly clipped his creative wings by imposing a site situated in the middle of a field, next to a railroad track, in a mainly working-class section of Šiška. Plečnik's ideal was no longer the modernization and adaptation of twentieth-century technology to the basilicas of the early Christians, but a new, monumental composition made up of classical elements and improved from a liturgical and practical point of view. He also worked at lowering the ceilings, so as to diminish the cost of construction and maintenance. His desire to assemble the faithful near the high altar was also new and represented a departure from Wagner's ideas about the altar's visibility. For Saint Francis Church, Plečnik placed the altar near the center of the square room. In the mid-twenties, Plečnik had begun to regard the pillar as a symbol of humanist tendencies in architecture, conceived as an ideological opposition to functionalism. This is why, shortly after his return from Prague, he said that it was difficult for him to live in a city without columns.

Though the plans for Saint Francis Church constituted a variation on a monumental sanctuary planned for Prague, the construction of which was suspended for a few years by strong liberal opposition, Plečnik imparted a new character to the building. He wanted its atmosphere to resemble that of the baroque Saint Trinity

Church, which had been influenced by Venice, and, because of its Palladian gravity, represented for him the still unequaled canon of the national architectural tradition. The novelty of Saint Francis Church also resided in the slightly raised "promenade" surrounding its central altar (perhaps inspired by a reproduction of the first basilica of Saint Peter's in Rome) that gave the impression of a great antique atrium. From a practical standpoint, its interest lay in the fact that a series of columns allowed for a more intimate participation in the service.

Plečnik's desire to be relatively isolated during the Mass, a desire brought on by middle age, played a considerable role in his projects for sacred architecture. This inclination was carried farthest in the crypt of the Franciscan church in Zagreb (1934–36), where he created an irregular arrangement of columns of varying widths. In Šiška, using purely architectonic means, he attempted to avoid the cumbersome decorations

that, by contributing undesirable sentimentality, would counteract his efforts to attain a stern monumentality. The usual round bell tower with its classical columns is the most explicit example of his symbolic and static architecture of the twenties (see "Portfolio" section).

Plečnik's first Slovenian church aroused heated debates. He was criticized for being un-Catholic, and the bishop's secretary, Josip Dostal, even succeeded in temporarily halting construction. If on the one hand, the design was too revolutionary for the conservative clergy, who were accustomed to pseudohistorical forms, on the other hand, the architect's students did not understand it. The cutting apart and then pasting together of the capitals and their columns was, for many of them, a veritable moral shock that rocked their unconditional faith in their master's creative principles.

Church of the Ascension, Bogojina

That same year, 1924, Plečnik received an unexpected commission: the expansion of the old parish church of Bogojina, in the region of Prekmurje, in Slovenia (see "Portfolio" section). Although he had trouble understanding the mentality of the clergy of Prekmurje, he studied this commission with growing interest, as the idea of preventing the demolition of the former church took shape. He reestablished a dialogue between the old and the new by adding to the wall of the medieval church, which had subsequently been treated in a baroque fashion, and transformed its interior into a porch, above which he built the organ loft of the great annex. Respect for the work of the local masons of the past also influenced Plečnik's plan for the new church. He adapted the width to the length of the old building, while making the two naves of different widths correspond to the baroque vault. Columns play an obvious role in the Bogojina church, but they are of smaller dimensions, relative to their environ-ment, than the elegant columns in Saint Francis Church. Using one of his old drawings from Vienna, Plečnik wove the space with arches of varying sizes, successfully limiting the severity of the classical architraves and creating a very expressive interior, comparable to the famous chapel of Ronchamp. Both architectures display an attempt at a plastic conception of the building; the only difference being that Plečnik, unseduced by new forms and the nearly unlimited plastic possibilities of concrete, remained faithful to traditional forms. For this reason he was extraordinarily pleased when the peasants of Bogojina chose, at the onset of construction in spring 1925, beautiful gray marble columns from Podpeč.

The desire to adapt to the milieu was a constant in Plečnik's sacred architecture. Even though the construction of the Bogojina church brought him a number of commissions in the Prekmurje region, he remained rather unfamiliar with this part of Slovenia.

Church of the Ascension, Bogojina, 1925–27

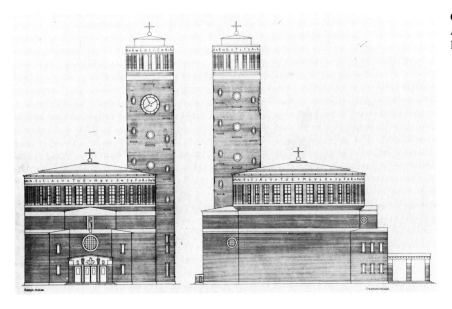

Church of Saint Anthony of Padua, Belgrade

The Church of Saint Anthony of Padua in Belgrade marked the beginning of Plečnik's study of sacred buildings with a central layout, which led him to extraordinarily interesting spatial and structural combinations. He was undoubtedly inspired by Belgrade's different cultural environment and its still vital tradition of medieval Serbian architecture. He paid only minor attention to the question of roofs, that is, to the vault of Saint Anthony Church, attending more closely to the building's interior space. Influenced by the idea that preparation is necessary for one's encounter with the high altar, he agreed to a compromise and used the suggested longitudinal axis.

In his series of projects for sacred places with central layouts that were never realized, we should make special note of the plans for Saint Joseph Cathedral in Sarajevo (1935). Plečnik envisaged it as a truncated cone surrounded by exterior flying buttresses and ending with a flat cupola. Since, except for his friend, the Franciscan Father Josip Markušić, he found no support in Bosnia for his project, he gave it to the Croatians during the war. When, after the liberation, the construction of a Parliament was on the agenda, he developed the basic principles of the monumental church for Bosnia into a project that he called, symbolically, "the cathedral of our freedom."

Saint Michael Church, Barje

Plečnik addressed the conception of smaller chapels with the same inventive talent, focusing principally on adapting them to their milieux. In 1937 he constructed Saint Michael Church in the "swamp" (Barje) of Ljubljana, upon the request of his nephew, the priest Karel Matkovič (see "Portfolio" section). He envisaged the body of the church in unpolished stone from Podpeč, without roughcast plaster. "You won't fool God with concrete," he told his nephew, who opposed his choice of foundation. Nevertheless,

Plečnik was unable to realize his vision to the end. On the ground floor, designed to house ecclesiastic apartments, the masons built a wall too regular for his taste. To correct this, he decided to build the upper floors in brick and stone. He found an original way to lower construction costs by placing concrete pipes such as those used for the city's distribution system between the masonry walls and filling in the gaps with wooden beams. Inside the church, he had these pipes polished and painted with colored motifs. Typologically, Saint Michael's is a room with an altar along its side wall. In designing the plans, Plečnik did not rely on popular Slovenian tradition; rather, the unusual interior is closer to the old, wooden sub-Caparthian churches he had observed in Czechoslovakia. An enclosed space, situated in the center of the church and designed for children so that their parents could watch them

during the Mass, is also one of Plečnik's innovations. If, within the church, it is not always possible to follow the genesis of different forms, the origin of the bell tower (built separately from the church because of the nature of the soil) has a far clearer significance: it monumentalizes simple elements—such as those used in place of the bell towers in the Karst region—by which Plečnik reminds us of his origins.

Although he had many opportunities while in Prague, Plečnik had no real contact with the court of the young Yugoslavian state. Yet, without knowing his nationality, King Alexander had shown enthusiasm for Plečnik's work. Plečnik paid no more than a short visit to Belgrade in 1927 and gave some minor advice during the construction of the new governmental residence; the king was probably too much of a military man and too uncultured, as the

Saint Michael Church, Barje, Ljubljana, 1937–38

Czechoslovakian president aptly noted. Plečnik carefully avoided the officials of Belgrade, and, despite the advice of certain Slovenian politicians, never produced anything "profane" in the state's capital. The royal Suvobor of Bled villa, which he was invited to build in 1924, also remained in the planning stages.

Plečnik's City Planning

In the mid-twenties three men presided over the destiny of Ljubljana: Plečnik, the engineer and director of city planning Matko Prelovšek, and France Stelé, an art historian. Many of their ideas were developed, spontaneously and without official approval, while they gathered around a glass of wine in the working-class inn Pri Kolovratu. At first, working with the gardener Anton Lap, Plečnik planted a few trees or repaired a neglected corner of the city with old blocks of stone found in the city's warehouses.

In 1927, under Plečnik's direction, the municipality undertook several tasks, including the restoration of Zoïs Street and of Šentjakob (Saint Jacob) Square, and the paving of the immense surface of the former Congress Square. Shortly afterward, Vegova Street was created along with the Illyrian monument (1929), the reconstruction of the Roman wall in Mirje (1928–38), and the restoration of the approaches to Šentflorijan (Saint Florian) Church (1930–35). Plečnik enriched the city with archaeological remains from the Roman Emona. He took great liberties in his plans to restore monuments; in the Roman wall that he saved from destruction, for example, we sense the memories of his voyage to Italy and his admiration for the funerary monuments of the Via Appia.

Plečnik installed only two great obelisks in Ljubljana: one in the form of an elegant column in memory of Napoleon's Illyrian provinces (1929), the other a colossal pillar produced in Tuscany by Vignole, on Saint Jacob Square (1938). In both cases placement was essential: the Illyrian monument marks the start of a lane planned as a unified whole, which was to lead to a series of propylaea; the pillar of Saint Jacob replaced a stella dedicated to the Virgin in the center of the former Jesuit square. He invested the Zoïs pyramid (1927) with a similar role, marking a break in the street's axis, while optically arresting the inclination of the terrain toward the Ljubljanica. The imposing stairway at the Garden of Paradise, in Prague, was the origin of a series of more modest projects, such as the stairway of Saint Florian Church (1932), the candelabras on the steps situated near the Philharmonic, and the surroundings of Saint Jerney Church in Šiška in 1938. Although Plečnik had studied with Italian architects the paving of squares using geometric forms, the passion he developed in Prague for the old way of paving—placing stones in sand—played an important role in his restoration of Ljubljana.

Unlike Max Fabiani, who, twenty years earlier, had focused on Ljubljana's vital functions, Plečnik attempted to awaken the national conscience with beauty and grandeur and to extirpate the last drops of serfdom still flowing in Slovenian veins. He paid less attention to the practical problems of the city, envisaging in the city's suburbs individual houses built on long and narrow sunny lots rather than great agglomerations. He took great care in establishing a plan for the rapidly expanding northern part of the city, Bežigrad, an area situated between the former Vienna Street, the railway tracks,

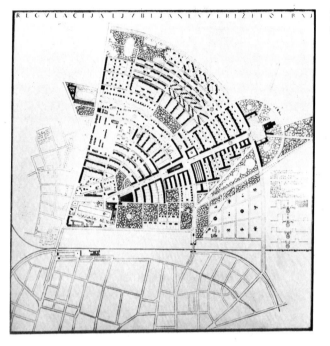

**Plan for the northern
section of Ljubljana,
1928**

and a large circular road that was being planned
and that, despite numerous compromises, was
not officially abandoned until the end of the
Second World War. He wanted to place the ac-
cent on a large avenue, along which a series of
cultural and administrative buildings would be
situated. This avenue would lead from the city's
old cemetery to its new one, thus symbolizing
the link between past, present, and future. The
dominant position of the castle, which over-
looks the old city of Ljubljana, had also long
attracted Plečnik; until 1932 he worked on a
vast restoration plan in which the building
would yield part of its historical identity to a
new cultural content. With the same enthusiasm as in Prague, he traced new paths of
communication between the city and the
castle's hill. But this vision appeared utopian,
and in the end Plečnik was able to realize only
the staircase and a few openings in the fortifica-
tions on the east side of the hill (1934).

Plečnik saw counterparts for Ljubljana castle in
Šiška Hill and Tivoli Park, situated below, where
he planned to erect several buildings: a national
gallery, a university, and a parliament with a reinforced concrete cone-shaped roof, rising more
than one hundred meters. Plečnik was concerned with landscaping the city as well, with
applying his botanical knowledge to the relationship between architecture and vegetation.
Just as he systematically replaced the traditional
chestnut with sycamore trees, which were
healthier and better adapted to the climate,
he replaced the city's existing vegetation with
carefully selected shrubbery. By his interventions, he not only preserved old trees, but also
through the use of climbing plants, protected
the roughcast concrete from humidity and rain.

In the center of the city, he paid great attention to the renovation of Južni Trg (South Square), between Zvezda Park and Čopova Street. In a competition for the royal monument, he completed his project with propylaea where the equestrian statue of the sovereign would be placed. The affair quickly became a major political issue, but despite new proposals by Plečnik the ensemble was never built.

In 1930 Plečnik was invited to participate in a project to deepen the Ljubljanica. The results of this collaboration were terraces planted with weeping willows the length of the port of Trnovo, Čevljarski Most (Shoemakers' Bridge), the Gerber stairway, Tromostovje (the Three Bridges), and the lock of Poljane. At the same time Plečnik restored the banks of the Gradaščica, over which he built two bridges. His dialogue with water went far beyond simple engineering. It inspired diverse ideas that frequently resulted in bold projects, such as the

construction of a convent or a city hall above the impetuous river. He also knew how to turn a bridge—a traditional meeting place—into a true market. Thus in Trnovo, he created an appropriate parvis for a parish church and made Čevljarski Most into a natural auditorium, for which the castle served as the romantic wings. His model for Mesarski Most (Butcher's Bridge) included a roof to protect pedestrians from the weather. In this respect, the trees of Trnovo Bridge were an even more original idea. Tromostovje served to preserve a monument, for in building the two lateral passageways for pedestrians, Plečnik salvaged the old stone bridge, built in the middle of the past century. The addition of concrete ornamentation ensured the maintenance of a particularly dynamic composition with rapidly changing perspectives.

The start of new public construction in Ljubljana awoke a certain optimism in Plečnik: the budget allocated for the restoration of the Chamber of Commerce for Crafts and Industry (1925–27) allowed him to demonstrate the high level of applied arts in Slovenia. The new staircase at the Chamber of Commerce is a hymn to the glory of marble from Podpeč and Hotavlje. It also celebrates the classical column that, while appearing in many of his constructions, was always adapted to suit each structure's particular quality (see "Portfolio" section).

In 1938 Plečnik undertook plans for the main office of a Catholic financial firm, the Vzajemna Zavarovalnica Insurance Company (see "Portfolio" section). For this project, as for the Chamber of Commerce, he was assisted by France Tomažič. This building was a significant link between the Zacherl house in Vienna and the National Library in Ljubljana, for it was in working on this project that Plečnik progressed from the structural and technical research characteristic of Wagner's circle to an architecture that speaks the language of texture. The gray stone and bright red bricks allowed for a more plastic treatment of the building's shell than would have been possible using polished granite. With a sure sense of rhythm, Plečnik repeated certain elements of his youthful masterpiece, the Zacherl house, yet gave the building an entirely different look. The intensely dynamic, avant-garde quality of the Zacherl house gives way here to a calm classicism, as brick cylinders replace fine granite joints.

In 1932–33 Plečnik remodeled the interior of a villa belonging to the engineer Matko Prelovšek (see "Portfolio" section). Due to the recent transformation of Prague Castle, this apartment is today one of the principal extant examples of interiors created by Plečnik. Despite its modern content, its whitewashed walls and great windowed surfaces, it is the apartment's representational function that predominates. The architect was convinced that his friend counted among the elite, who should display their social position, and during his frequent visits to Prelovšek's home, he enjoyed verifying the results of his research. In matters of furnishings, he was more interested in the dignified posture of the body than in comfort.

National University Library
The National University Library in Ljubljana is undoubtedly one of the finest achievements of Plečnik's artistic maturity, intended to become a kind of national temple of knowledge and culture (see "Portfolio" section). This explains the entryway—long, dark, and lined with imposing columns—which leads to the large, bright reading rooms. Plečnik's conception of the entryway as sacred was already apparent in the Zacherl house, but he had been unable there to fully develop this idea. He did so in Ljubljana, where the entire intermediary wing is given over to the "ceremonial aisle."

In his plans, Plečnik intended to fill in the gap between Vergova Street and Gosposka Street resulting from the destruction of the late-Renaissance Auersperg Palace in the earthquake of 1895. In a desire for historical legitimacy, he planned to preserve the same volume as the preceding building, and applied used stones to the facade. Initially, this was more a matter of urban planning than of historical typology. On the exterior, the correlation between National University Library and the Zacherl house is evident. His search for the aesthetic qualities of materials—he had said that he had tried to monumentalize the Karst building by use of the mixed stone and brick structure apparent in the walls—led Plečnik to an interplay of pure textures. He limited his use of supporting columns to the symbolic decoration of the two large reading-room windows and allowed the plastic quality and color of the materials to express themselves freely. He thereby alleviated the compositional tensions between the horizontal and the vertical and softened the upper wall with a delicate decorative wreath, the shadow of which continues onto the smooth surface of the stone. The windows that project outward and the extraordinarily large statue of Moses are obvious reminders of the architect's Viennese years.

In the Ljubljana library, Plečnik's inner turmoil became more and more apparent. On three occasions he ripped out a main door that was organically related to the body of the rationally planned building. The same thing happened with the candelabras of the peristyle, for which, as for the lights of the Zacherl house stairway, he bore the consequences of his faithfulness to the Secession. The return to certain early themes in his art and the new use of "technoid" decoration, which we no longer see in the insurance company building or in the Bank of Celje (built during the same period), show that Plečnik was trying to incorporate all his knowledge and experience into his most important works. In this respect, the doors to the library's exhibition rooms are particularly remarkable.

Two factors were decisive in Plečnik's Ljubljana construction in the mid-thirties: the four-year-long preparation of a new plan for the city, which addressed the future of the architect's propositions, and the election of a mayor favorable to Plečnik. The time was right and projects were planned, such as the Slovenian Pantheon, Hram Slave (never built), on the site of the abandoned Saint Christopher cemetery. In the years preceding the war, Plečnik devoted all his attention to the construction of a new City Hall, a market, and to the renovation of the municipal cemetery.

The marketplace where the great high school building had once stood attracted him as had the gap caused by the earthquake at the site of the future National University Library. The result of his preoccupation were the plans for City Hall. The war prevented its being built,

National University Library, Ljubljana, 1936–41, detail of facade

**The "Fer à repasser,"
Ljubljana, 1932–34**

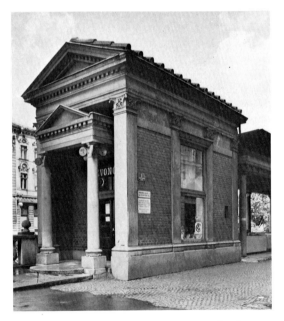

**Flower shop in the
Ljubljana market, 1941**

and today only the Renaissance-inspired forms of the nearby "Fer à repasser" ("Iron" building, 1933) remind us of its design. At the beginning of Poljanska Street, on a narrow, slanted parcel of land, Plečnik built, for the pleasure of experimentation, a building containing a staircase that, by an optical illusion, seems to go on indefinitely. To understand the market, we must view it as part of a unified conception including City Hall. Initially, Plečnik recommended a different site for this ensemble, but he finally placed it on the banks of the Ljubljanica, which he lined with elegantly curved columns. Two colonnades symmetrically soften the long bodies of buildings, in the middle of which he intended to add Butcher's Bridge.

Žale: Ensemble of Funerary Chapels

The rapid growth of Ljubljana soon made the growing number of funeral processions troublesome. In the hope of preserving the traditional farewell to the dead and at the same time avoiding the frightening atmosphere of big-city morgues, Plečnik proposed an ensemble of chapels, named for the city's patron saints, scattered throughout a garden (see "Portfolio" section). The last, dedicated to humanity's ancestors, was intended for nonbelievers or for those of different faiths. He made this ensemble of farewell chapels into a veritable city of the dead in which whiteness and solemnity preside, and all details are carefully planned, including a fountain, benches, tombstones, stretchers, and the uniforms of the employees, with their wide-rim hats. Plečnik's All-Saint's Garden, later prosaically called Žale, is a model of timeless architecture. Wherever possible Plečnik tried to adapt the functional buildings—for autopsies, for a caretaker, and for workshops to build coffins—to the symbolic intention of the site.

Žale cemetery,
Ljubljana, 1938–40,
chapel

Žale cemetery, chapel

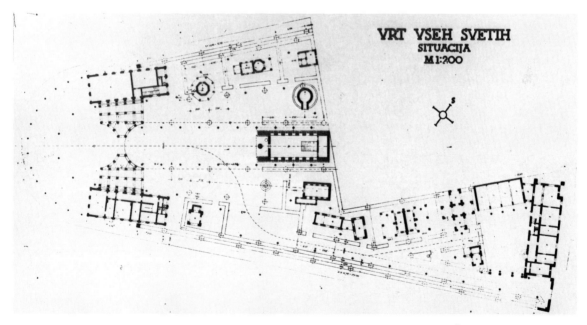

Žale cemetery, plan of
the City of the Dead

The powerful triumphal arch that separates this world from the world beyond is a pure, strictly classical architectural form animated by varied rhythms and spatial emphases. The chapels comprise a veritable encyclopedia of building styles, all derived from basic geometric shapes, interspersed, however, with a series of free forms that are difficult to classify. But another aspect of Žale is of greater importance: in the spirit of Semper or Wagner, Plečnik undertook to resolve the eternal architectural questions regarding the wall, or better, the "skin" of the building, the support structure, windows, roofs, light, and so on—the classic architectonic grammar that new materials and new technology had placed in a position of secondary importance.

Final Years

The war years could not contain the artist's creative drive. The less chance he had of actually building a project, the more his concepts became idealized. For years he presided over all of Ljubljana from his drawing table. He designed monumental lanes leading to the castle, with great votive sanctuaries, an Odéon at the end of Congress Square, a building for the Academy of Arts and Science, which was to return Novi Trg to its pre-earthquake appearance, the Saint Family Church in Moste, and a new theater; he thought about enlarging the National Museum and about organizing the former Virgin Mary Square, while constantly returning to his idea for a square in the south.

Aware that time was running out and that it would no longer be possible to protect the idyllic provincial appearance of the Krakovo suburb against real estate speculators, at the end of 1943 Plečnik presented a project called "house

under a municipal roof." Within certain restrictions, each person could build a suitable house in this socialist city, while the commune would build a collective roof, just as if it were constructing public works.

When the Germans closed the University of Ljubljana, Plečnik brought drafting materials to his home and continued holding classes. He did not lack work, since at the beginning of the war he still had many commissions for sacred buildings, especially for the Croatian religious orders. One reason for this is that he never billed anyone: it seemed immoral to him to receive money outside of his professor's salary. Despite this, his greatest ideas remained on paper (the monastery and Holy Cross Church in Zagreb [1939–49]; the surroundings of the pilgrimage church of Marija Bistrička [1942–43]). It is likely that Plečnik could at least have produced the monumental ensemble for the Jesuit monastery in Osijek, the first stone for which was laid in October 1940. The church had reached a height of eight meters when it became apparent that it could not be finished. During construction, the architect modified the plans and placed the monks' cells in a high tower, hiding an extraordinarily audacious construction beneath a neoclassical appearance.

Contrary to expectations, the end of the war did not bring work to Plečnik, but he and his students continued to model an ideal Ljubljana. At the height of his research, studies were produced for the Slovenian Parliament at the castle and for Tivoli Park (1947).

The restoration of the Stranje church, near Kamnik (1947–50), profaned during the war, gave the architect new energy. When he learned of the enthusiasm of the peasants, who set to work with no real technical direction, he was

**Pavilion for President
Tito, Brioni, 1956**

immediately ready to work on the project. He kept his ideas to himself, allowing the talent of the local craftspeople to dominate, and learned interesting variations on classical and folkloric styles. The Stranje church is above all an ensemble of rich elements, close in their manner of expression to the mind of the simple man. The transformation of an unused space under the bell tower into a baptistry earned him tremendous popularity. Subsequently, and until his death, he designed many baptistries for the churches of the Ljubljana diocese.

The official recognition he received from the religious community in the form of the Prešeren Award in 1949 strengthened Plečnik's delicate situation at the Technical School, where some of his former students were now in charge. In the euphoria of the pseudo-Le Corbusier trend that had taken belated control of Slovenian architecture, Plečnik obviously had no place. But his renewed popularity was apparent in the many commissions, from all parts of Slovenia, for monuments to those who had died for national liberation. The final link in this chain is the pavilion for President Tito, situated on one of the Brioni islands, designed shortly before the architect's death. Here Plečnik returned to the ideals of his youth, to Theodoric's monolithic cupolas in Ravenna and to the sculptured beams he had created for the Zacherls' music room. He reworked these elements into an ensemble in which architecture and sculpture organically mingle.

After the war, one of the few large commissions he received from the city was the restoration of a former monastery of the order of German Chevaliers (Križanke), which had been extremely neglected. The project began without him, but as no one really knew what to do with it, the eighty-year-old architect proposed transforming the courtyard into an open-air theater

and began drawing up the plans with indefatigable imagination. In the monastery's courtyard he placed many elements similar to those of Prague Castle: a pergola, varied pavements, arcades, vases, candelabras, and especially the lights he had used in the third courtyard. Perhaps inspired by the enclosures of Muslim cemeteries, Plečnik pierced windows in the wall of the former monastery to create links with the city. Križanke also became a kind of architectural "preserve," in which the old artist enclosed fragments of Ljubljana houses that had been destroyed, giving them new life in a new context, in the midst of an unbridled modernist current.

Plečnik's untiring creativity continued until his death. At the age of eighty-two he participated in a competition for the War Ministry in Belgrade. Until his final day he worked on the restoration of churches in Šiška, Bogojina, Belgrade, and Barje, and pondered over the completion of Žale, in Ljubljana, a work for which he remained more or less alone and misunderstood. "An absolutely new generation is coming of age while I appear to be fading in the dusk," he complained to his nephew Karel. In the mid-fifties, Slovenian architecture turned to northern Europe. Trade journals were filled with admiration for Scandinavian kitchens, new furnishings, and industrial production. It was in such an atmosphere that Plečnik died, peacefully, on January 6, 1957, in the house he had restored without any modern conveniences, amid the innumerable memories of his long life of creativity. True to himself until the very end, he had his own funerary monument built during his lifetime, so as to spare his family any unnecessary expense.

Pavilion in Begunje,
c. 1939

Plečnik in Brioni in
1956

Renovation of the
former Monastery of
the German Knights,
Ljubljana, 1950–56

Jože Plečnik and Prague

Vladimir Šlapeta

Today I read quite a few letters that I had received from Plečnik since the beginning of our friendship—letters from our student days, letters from his travels, letters that talk about his work during difficult periods, as well as during easier times. Such unity throughout! His mood varies of course, but the image remains essentially the same. That of a man who has a fixed goal and who advances toward it with a will of iron, conscious of each step he takes, subjecting his progression to unwavering self-criticism. He does not allow himself to be stopped by disappointment, or even—and this is more uncommon still—by worldly success. He remains oblivious to the rocky terrain, focusing only on the long road ahead. He and his art appear before my eyes. I remember how he progressed at a sustained and rapid pace, despite the battles and deprivation. Already in 1895, at the Academy of Vienna, the young, modest Slovenian student quickly attracted attention. He was not immediately liked by all his fellow students, united around Otto Wagner. His meditative nature distinguished him from those who enthusiastically and unquestioningly followed the path traced by their master; he did not share their joy at the precursors of modernity, and yet he himself was among the first of the moderns, a model for many.[1]

It was in these words that Jan Kotěra, a Czech friend and fellow student of Plečnik's at the Wagnerschule, introduced the works of Plečnik in 1902, in the journal *Volné Směry* (Free Tendencies), published by the Mánes artistic circle, of which he was president at the time. But this was not Plečnik's first contact with Czech culture. In his adolescence in Ljubljana he attentively read the literary and artistic reviews that appeared in Bohemia and studied the glorious past of the Czech people, whom he respected and considered the elite of the Slavic world.[2] In Otto Wagner's studio, the Slavic origins of both Plečnik and Kotěra drew them together. They were among Wagner's best students, and both received the Academy of Vienna's highest distinction, the Prix de Rome: Kotěra in 1897, Plečnik one year later. Mutual esteem for each other's work cemented their friendship, which lasted a lifetime. In 1898, at the age of twenty-seven, Kotěra was appointed professor at the School of Decorative Arts; he thus returned to Prague, where, as a teacher and organizer, he became the dominant figure in the Czech art world. He kept Plečnik informed about events in Bohemia, sent him the journal *Volné Směry* and, later on, *Styl*.[3] He also presented the work of Plečnik to the Czech people, mentioning him in *Volné Směry* for the first time in 1900, in the context of an article-manifesto entitled "On the New Art," illustrated with reproductions of works by the most important European architects.

At times critical, at times admiring, Plečnik comments on these events in his correspondence. When a special issue of *Volné Směry* appeared, dedicated to the Czech symbolist sculptor František Bílek,[4] whose dreamy, poetic, and profoundly religious expression Plečnik admired, he wrote to Kotěra:

I was very enthusiastic about the Bílek issue, his works are fascinating. Wagner was surprised, and said that he wanted to subscribe to the journal, but I don't know if he really meant it. If you like, and if the occasion arises, tell all this to Mr. Bílek; also send him my sincerest thanks for his great genius. May God be with you.[5]

A few years later, when Kotěra published pictures of Plečnik's Zacherl house, of Berlage's Stock Exchange in Amsterdam, and of his own works[6] in *Volné Směry*, Plečnik wrote to him:

Berlage made me very happy. Especially because we are similar: I first wanted to do the Zacherl house in brick—differently of course—but I was laughed at. I find it unfortunate that we so rarely hear the word "brick" these days. There are many good things in Berlage's work, but the vertical solution to the main area is not entirely convincing. What I like most is the entrance to the great hall (last picture). I find the facade of your house a bit weak, but the staircase is fantastic, and the most successful project is the conference room at the Town Hall by Jindřichův Hradec. The second burial vault (on the right) for the Vojan family that you did with Sucharda is very, very beautiful. And speaking of this great

Letter from Plečnik to Jan Kotěra

master, Sucharda, for once his contribution leaves me cold.[7] Excuse me—I don't mean to be critical—it is so difficult to talk about artistic work. Basically I would say that the idea for the interior was not carried to its conclusion. One of the new faces from whom I expect a great deal is Gočár—he seems to me quite capable of following your example—or am I wrong about him? You also could have included a few plans, even in a small format, but never mind. The thing that impressed me most in the entire issue was your text: your views are constantly expanding! Only it is unfortunate that for my tastes—and I have so much confidence in you—at times you lack a touch of melancholy.[8]

This mention of Josef Gočár is the first show of interest in the young cubist generation of Czech architects[9]; these architects, students of Kotěra, developed warm ties with Plečnik in the early 1900s. The judgment made here turns out to be well-founded. Upon the death of Kotěra, it is Gočár who replaced him as chair of the Academy of Fine Arts in Prague. In another letter, Plečnik speaks with equal perspicacity of Pavel Janák, who was twice to become his successor,[10] "Master Janák is without doubt an excellent artist, and probably also an excellent man, but for now I am not entirely certain that he is not more competent as a reporter, a chronicler or, say, a critic."[11] As a theoretician, Janák would indeed be the driving spirit of the cubist movement in Prague. If Gočár, thanks to the soundness of his expressive means, was to become the principal creator of the new Czech architecture, Janák proved the most inspirational, experimental, and probably the best teacher. Plečnik met them both before 1910: Janák upon a visit to Wagner's studio[12] and Gočár by way of Jan Kotěra.

Gočár and Janák took part in the founding the journal *Styl*, which began to appear in 1908. Janák used this forum to formulate his critique of Wagner's teachings. In a manifesto entitled *From Modern Architecture to Architecture*,[13] he promulgated the importance of discovering the spiritual in matter—rather than the function—by means of a plastic approach to form. When *Styl* published documents on Wagner's Church am Steinhof,[14] Plečnik sent the editorial board an indignant letter:

The ensemble gives the impression of a Protestant church, of an oratory, of a choir, but not of a [Catholic] church. Yet it all corresponds to Wagner's ideas: "a nonconfessional style, an undetermined faith, changing each day in step with one's mood." Hollow grandiloquence. Indistinct, a crossbreed; the provocative absence of all conviction. We sense the frivolous desire to finish hastily, to put an end to the principles of all times and all ages. This man has had success his entire life, has joyfully skipped over the world's eternal rules, which is why he has become unworthy of grace, he has lost contact with the people, he does not understand their souls or their needs, he has no sense for what is most sacred in people, for what we succinctly call God. This is his reward. Upon looking at this work, I say to myself: better to have no art at all than an art of this nature. I understand why the ancients built so slowly—oh, they had a conscience, for them, it was all a saintly affair, as is proven by the mystical traditions that have been perpetuated to this day. Modern men work without a conscience; yes, we work more quickly, but I doubt that future generations will remember us with the respect that we, thank God, owe to the ancients.[15]

While Janák emphasizes the power of the spirit, Plečnik above all appreciates moral conscience.

The next issue of *Styl* carried a text on Plečnik's recent works. The artist is described in these terms:

His originality is incontestable, although his intro- verted nature does not facilitate access to the roots of this originality, and we have only a limited body of work from which to judge. . . . Plečnik is a very whole individual, very exclusive in his art; his relationship to contemporary life is full of misunderstanding and sorrow. Creatively, he is con- sumed with producing variations on one same idea, which he submits to a profound reflection for each occasion. The key to his character and to his creative activity is a quasi-ascetic rigor, dictated by a pro- found and authentic religious conviction that he imposes both on those around him and above all on himself. Plečnik is a believer whose creative production is determined by his faith. His artistic individuality is also characterized by asceticism and by the sincerity of his convictions; his faith demands an extreme honesty, causing him to constantly ques- tion the value of his work. Due to the constraint of this self-critique, Plečnik can only create slowly and painfully; he attempts to clarify the logic of each detail, and it is only after having elaborated each and every element, in what might appear to be an excessively meticulous fashion, that he moves toward the completion of a work. A harsh, unforgiving logic, an in-depth analysis of the task at hand, a quest for the means and the forms suitable to its architectonic expression—all this often imposes difficult obstacles for an artist with a fertile imagi- nation whose capacity to express itself is, in other respects, exceptional. Just as the baroque artist, using all the tools of his trade and all the nuance of his talent, created an impressive ensemble, a pictur- esque silhouette, so Plečnik submits function to an implacable critique, condemning the subordination of form to utility. Just as the baroque architect did not concern himself with the rules governing centuries- old elements, but used them as he pleased provided they suited his conception, so Plečnik does not worry about the origins or stylistic stamp of his details. The decisive factor is not for him the form as such, but its logic and intention. Thus we find historical elements juxtaposed without the slightest interest in history, brought in simply because they lend them- selves to his goal. When Plečnik has recourse to new forms and new technologies, these too are the logical result of extensive reflection, without any of the contingency attached to innovation for the sake of innovation. Where another architect might use artifice freely, Plečnik's use of form is arrived at fol- lowing a prolonged meditation, during which he might weigh the pros and cons hundreds of times. When others imitate his methods, the results are weak and disappointing, for the road leading to them is not the same. It is rare for such an artist to find support among the masses, and Plečnik is no exception. His projects, even his most extensive ones, remain for the most part in the form of sketches; never built, they have, for all intents and purposes, no influence on the development of architecture and on public opinion. This eminent talent remains without an echo, which is all the more regrettable as the modern school can boast of only a handful of such original artists.[16]

When, the following year, *Styl* reproduced two of Plečnik's church projects,[17] the groundwork was laid for his welcome to Prague. Certain of his sketches[18] exercised an incontestable influ- ence on the evolution of cubist architecture in Prague, notably on the work of Pavel Janák. But the professorship at the School of Decorative Arts, obtained for him by his old friend Jan Kotěra, gave him the opportunity to shape a new generation of Czech architects.

In 1910 Kotěra founded an architecture studio within the Academy of Fine Arts in Prague and turned over his chair at the School of Decorative Arts to Plečnik. Plečnik gratefully accepted and wrote to Kotěra, "I think—and I am telling you this today—that insofar as the destiny of a man depends on his peers, I put my fate in your hands."[19] He left Vienna for Prague, and on January 20, 1911, officially assumed responsibility for the architecture section at the School of Decorative Arts.[20] Thus in the 1910s the Czech capital possessed two schools of architecture directed by two great authorities, both from the school of Otto Wagner. Kotěra, *"grand seigneur,"*[21] man of the world, led his students toward modern rationalism, thus forming the

first functionalist generation to follow the cubists. Plečnik, on the other hand, a strong but introverted personality, concentrated his teaching on the classical heritage of Mediterranean architecture, which had attracted him since his youth.[22] His inner religious sentiment was also reflected in his pedagogical activity. As Josef Štěpánek, one of the best students, remembered the school: "The religious atmosphere, the fervent Catholic attachment to chapels and dimly lit recesses, submission to mysticism and to the typographical beauty of the Latin language, all this created a sea of spiritualism in which the students immersed themselves."[23] Upon the death of his master, in 1957, Štěpánek wrote, "It was clear to all that the new professor was investing his life here and sacrificing his private life and happiness."[24] Another student, Jindřich Merganc, wrote to Plečnik from Bratislava, almost forty years after leaving the school: "Your exemplary life and your art will always shine in my memory, dear professor, which is why I remembered you at each crossroad of my existence."[25]

Plečnik's attitude toward his students was full of paternal generosity. His diligence, his intransigent demands, the quality and the strength of his views on art, his rigorous justice, and the austerity of his life provided an exemplary model. He was repaid by the devotion and admiration of his students. While Kotěra's teaching was liberal and tolerated a plurality of directions, Plečnik's school possessed an almost dogmatic unity of expression. Profane subjects were put aside to focus on monumental, sacred, and funerary themes, all treated in the spirit

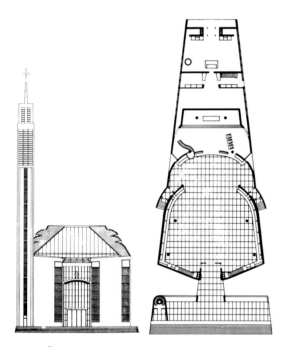

**Josef Štěpánek,
project for a church,
Brno-Zidenice**

of antiquity.[26] If Plečnik was unhappy with the work of a student, he often helped to resolve the problem by producing a sketch himself.[27] Otakar Novotný, a student of Kotěra who taught at the School of Decorative Arts beginning in 1929, was critical of his pedagogical methods:

Plečnik helps by intervening directly in his students' projects, which weakens their capacities for judgment. It is a manner of teaching that leaves no visible trace. In time, his students give up the little they were able to perceive of Plečnik's grandeur, and elect to follow Kotěra's teachings rather than those of their own master,[28] who nonetheless gave them the basis for a grandiose conception, made them attentive to detail, and refined their taste in the expression of ideas. Unfortunately, all this was unrelated to the preoccupations of the day, and had no real living content. We are therefore forced to conclude that this grand artist was basically only an episodic character in the evolution of Czech architecture.[29]

Among Plečnik's forty-nine Czech students, a number went on to notable careers. Perhaps the most gifted among them, Karel Faulhammer, was killed in the war, but Otto Rothmayer, a longtime colleague of Plečnik, distinguished himself by his personal contributions to Prague Castle and played an important role in Czech architecture during the period between the two world wars.[30] The same can be said of Josef Fuchs, Ludvík Hilgert, Karel Řepa, and Josef Štěpánek,[31] who developed functionalist conceptions, as well as of František L. Gahura in Zlín and of Jindřich Merganc in Slovakia.[32] Alois Mezera became known for his crematorium in the Prague cemetery of Strašnice and for his Czech embassies in Ankara, Berlin,

Belgrade, and Varsovy[33]; Alois Metalák gained recognition as a designer of glass works[34]; and Karel Štipl was known for his plastic decors.[35] Other architects also claim Plečnik as their guiding influence. Among them are Bedřich Feuerstein,[36] who consulted him privately in parallel to his studies at the Polytechnic School, and, of course, Pavel Janák, a faithful admirer who wrote to him, "I love this great and ancient art so. Many times when I take pictures and I see it before me (I learn so much!), I remember you, your deep and beautiful understanding of it, like no one else's in the world! And you're so skilled at it, just like the ancients."[37]

Plečnik produced few architectural projects during the second decade of the century. During the difficult period of World War I and the years immediately preceding it, he felt it would be wrong to compete with Czech architects.[38] A few chalices and other religious instruments, a monument at the Křivoklát cemetery (1911–12), and sketches for the monument of Šiška (1913)[39] are the only traces of Plečnik's activity in Prague before 1920. He devoted himself to the publication of his students' works, however, encouraging them to become independently active by introducing them to the public.[40]

The foundation of the first Czech republic finally gave Plečnik the opportunity to realize his ideas in Prague. In 1919 and 1920, Kotěra attempted to establish a second chair in architecture at the Academy of Fine Arts[41] for the benefit of his friend, but the project never came to fruition.[42] Pedagogically, Plečnik was already on the road home to his native country. On

April 1, 1921, he left the School of Decorative Arts in Prague (having resigned on January 21, 1921[43]), to assume responsibility for the architecture studio at the newly founded University of Ljubljana, a position to which he was appointed during the winter semester of 1920–21. But the greatest work of his Prague period was yet to be accomplished. In 1919 Jan Kotěra had created the interior of the first apartment for President Tomás G. Masaryk at Prague Castle.[44] Kotěra had Plečnik named castle architect, thereby entrusting him with the task of its reconstruction, to which Masaryk gave his approval. Plečnik's love for the antique coincided with his concept of a democratic state, founded on humanist ideals. The designation of a representative from an allied Slovenian nation as castle architect symbolized the political idea of pan-Slavism: the alliance between the peoples of Czechoslovakia and of Yugoslavia, who had just overthrown the yoke of the Hapsburg monarchy. These two events—his appointment at the University of Ljubljana and at Prague Castle—mark a turning point in Plečnik's life. Henceforth, he spent most of the year at Ljubljana, teaching and setting up projects both for his native city and for Prague Castle, returning to Bohemia each summer to personally survey the work on the castle, where his student Otto Rothmayer replaced him during his absence. The careers of Kotěra and Plečnik also diverge at this point, separating two loyal friends who were so different in nature: one, a man of the world, the other, melancholy and ascetic. Until the end, Plečnik remained grateful to his Czech friend. In his last letter of December 15, 1921, when Kotěra had but a little over a year left to live, Plečnik wrote to him in Czech:

Dear and highly esteemed friend! A different mentality, a different career, all this separates us according to the laws of nature, it is true. But it is also true that something better still unites us: your generous heart and my gratitude. We are both now on the threshold of a new existence. On this momentous occasion we must remember to thank the Lord; and as we look ahead, may God help us! May that be enough![45]

In his work at Prague Castle, Jože Plečnik interpreted in a new and original manner the *genius loci* of this historical and architectonic complex (see "Portfolio" section). He reworked the courtyards, terraces, gardens, and recesses[46] in keeping with his grandiose conception, imposing order and monumentality, but also a Mediterranean atmosphere of intimacy and contemplation, an architecture of memories. Plečnik drew on the classical order of antiquity, enlivening it with a specifically Slavic touch. He treated the interiors similarly: the president's apartment[47] and especially the monumental pillared entrance, later called the Plečnik Room. A perfectionist, he worked with exemplary professional honesty, using beautiful natural materials, brick, metal, wood, and especially stone, chosen from Czech mines.[48] "If there were enough money," he liked to say, "I would build a castle entirely of stone. I would get the greatest pleasure from it. Even the doors could be made of stone. You don't believe me? We could so do by making them of marble plaques that pivot in the center."[49] Yet this work was undertaken at a time when Czech architecture was focused on extremely different problems: freeing itself from postwar cubism, distancing

Prague Castle, Garden on the Ramparts, the pergola and granite table

Prague Castle,
one of the two pine
flagpoles in front of
Mathias Gate in the
first courtyard

Prague Castle,
the granite beam in
front of the obelisk
in the Garden on the
Ramparts

**Prague Castle,
stairway leading to the
Garden of Paradise**

**Prague Castle,
pyramid in the Garden
on the Ramparts**

itself from the richly ornamented "national style,"[50] and orienting itself toward civic art, the new objectivity, and constructivism.[51] It was a paradox to which Pavel Janák was not insensitive:

Down below, the struggle for a way of thinking and building, the search for a single, universally valid conception that can be imposed and defended against all other possibilities, that would be applicable everywhere, that would be beyond questioning. Up here [that is, at the castle] an artist who simply builds, as if he had not the slightest doubt as to what he was doing: the exact opposite of the work being done down below, heading not only in a different direction, but in an entirely personal one. Down below, they are seeking the most rational and most economical mode of construction possible. Up here is an artist who seems unaware of the price of materials, whose appreciation for them increases with their rarity, who specifically chooses the best and the most expensive among them. Down below, they are interested only in necessity and in justification. The artist here is lost in meditation on the proportions of columns. Down below we hear: "numbers, activity, organization, finances, utility, profitability." Here we have an art full of modesty and devotion.[52]

In addition to working on the president's apartment at Prague Castle, Plečnik also attended to the restoration of Masaryk's summer residence in Lány, where his most important architectural contribution was the dam at the Lány hunting grounds.

During the reconstruction work, Plečnik became interested in the urban context of the castle and its grounds. On several occasions— in 1921, 1922, and 1928[53]—he sought a means of access to the castle starting from Mánes

Bridge. In the late twenties, he conceived of a new monumental entryway to the castle's grounds, originating at the Fossé aux Cerfs. A broad, winding path would lead from the depths of the fosse to the summit, beneath the Queen Anne Pavilion. Here we would find the new entrance, covered by a bridge linking the Belvedere to the Dalibor Tower and the Black Tower. In the early thirties, the architect pursued his studies of the relationship between the castle and its urban surroundings and envisioned changes to the northern border of the complex.

In the first half of the twenties Plečnik's work was favorably received by the public. The changes made to the main courtyard, to the president's apartment, and to the gardens were considered a great success, and the architect received many awards,[54] but his projects later met with disapproval. The paving of the third courtyard was opposed with increasing vehemence when he made public his project for access by way of the Fossé aux Cerfs, and it culminated in a hostile campaign against the adaptation of the northern side, which was to be crowned by the construction of the Masaryk Library. Action was undertaken by the Society of Friends of Old Prague, which, with the assistance of several other artistic and cultural associations, organized an inquiry into Plečnik's project. The result was a resolution that declared it "unfeasible, as it represents an attempt against the thousand-year-old evolution of the Castle and its grounds."[55] The society of Friends of Old Prague had no qualms about publishing a highly critical and chauvinist text in its newsletter, signed by 245 Czech women:

We have so many excellent Czech architects who would lovingly and patriotically take charge of the necessary adaptations without harming the monument left to us by our ancestors. We are now allowing a foreign architect, using a foreign style, and with neither love nor sensitivity for our historical monuments, to do what the former hostile government did not do. The women of the Czech Republic beg of you: Save our Castle.[56]

These violent and disloyal attacks are probably what pushed Plečnik to resign from his post as castle architect. He made no subsequent trips to Prague in 1935[57] and never realized his plans for the Deep Park, for the prolongation of the northern side, for the tennis courts, and for the Royal Garden. "The tennis courts and the Royal Garden," he said, "are the most beautiful architectonic poem of Central Europe. There is no greater task than that of adapting them."[58] In 1936 his great admirer, Pavel Janák, replaced him.[59]

The final architectural creation of Jože Plečnik's Prague period takes place outside of the castle. It is only by hearsay that we know of his idea to prolong Venceslas Square beyond the Můstek intersection, toward Rytířská Street, all the way to the Municipal Savings Building,[60] but the Sacred Heart Church, in the Vinohrady quarter, represents one of his best works in the domain of sacred architecture. He received the commission under exceptional circumstances. On April 4, 1919, the Prague Architecture Society sent Plečnik a letter bearing the signature of twenty-nine of its prominent members:

Honored Professor! Having deliberated over the competition currently being prepared for the construction of a second Catholic Church in Vinohrady, our association has arrived at the conviction that

**Sacred Heart Church,
Prague**

this competition could produce nothing better and more authentic than a work created by you. We have long been hoping that Prague would one day be enriched with a work of your hands, a work that we are certain would constitute one of its greatest jewels. Consequently, we suggested to the society organizing the competition that the competition be canceled and that we entrust the work directly to you. We are now informed that it is too late to cancel the public competition, but the jury suggests that we ask you to submit a project hors-concours. *We are therefore unanimously requesting that you undertake this task under these conditions. We assure you that we are asking this out of common accord, in all sincerity, and with the hope that you will not refuse.*[61]

For the Czech architects, this was a way of thanking Plečnik for his pedagogical activity in Prague, a reward that preceded his appointment as castle architect. Plečnik yielded to his colleagues' insistence only after much hesitation. In his initial project, in which the sanctuary was surrounded by the Doric peristyle, he placed the bell tower separately. It is only in the last two versions that his forty-two-meter-high tower took its distinctive stele-like form, an enlarged symbol of the tabernacle. Yet the church's main architectural contribution, which Plečnik created between 1928 and 1932, shortly before the end of his Prague period, is its interior. Its inner space, conceived of in imposingly large dimensions, anticipates the concept that became the norm ten years or so later following the Vatican II council. Plečnik invested it with an ardent atmosphere of spiritual devotion. The church was consecrated

on May 8, 1932, less than three years before Plečnik left Prague permanently. It represents his final important contribution to the Czech capital.

Jože Plečnik worked in Prague regularly from 1911 to 1921 and was present there until 1935 because of his work on the castle. Thanks to Jan Kotěra, his works were regularly published in Bohemia starting in 1900. Plečnik had both good and bad moments, but his lack of concern for personal success enabled him to remain unaffected by them. Is it then accurate to characterize him as an "episodic character" in the evolution of Czech architecture? It is true that during the period between the world wars most Bohemian architects, in their enthusiasm for the international avant-garde, followed other paths; it is also true that, among his own disciples, very few (Alois Mezera, Otto Rothmayer, Karel Štipl, Alois Metalák) remained faithful to his teachings.[62] Yet all of his students recognized his artistic and moral authority; on the occasion of his fiftieth birthday, some wrote: "In the history of art it would be difficult to find an example of someone who combines genius with humanity and pedagogical aptitude such as they are found in Jože Plečnik."[63] Even after more than half a century, the architectural heritage he left in Prague—at the castle and in the Vinohrady quarter—still do not belong to the past. His strong and original message concerns the future as well as the present. The current generation is sensitive to the courage with which this artist was able to resist the ephemeral preoccupations of the moment and to devote himself entirely to the supreme problems of architectural creation. Still hesitant in his youth, it is only at the end of his Viennese period that Plečnik attained the equilibrium of the classical architectonic order. In Prague he proved grandiose and monumental, in keeping with the themes of castle and church. His final period in his native Ljubljana is marked by a singularly intimate atmosphere, by a contemplative and dreamy, distinctly Slavic tonality, by which he renews the forms of classical architecture as well as those of the Slovenian tradition. The unity in his work is achieved by consistently placing moral values above aesthetic considerations, and it is in this respect that his heritage is not "episodic" but fundamental. "If I want to create good architecture," he used to say, "I must be a good man."[64] Good architecture was for him, first and foremost, the humble, devoted, and sincere serving of humanity and society, conceived as *sub specie aeternitatis*. "Friend," he writes in a letter to his student Josef Štěpánek, "tell yourself often that you are what you are not by the grace of man, but by the grace of God, and you'll see that you'll find life much easier."[65]

■ Notes

1. *Volné Směry* 6 (Prague, 1902), p. 91.

2. D. Prelovšek, *Josef Plečnik, Wiener Arbeiten von 1896 bis 1914* (Vienna: Tusch, 1979), p. 53.

3. The journal *Styl* began appearing in 1908.

4. The issue devoted to František Bílek appeared in 1900 (vol. 4, pp. 113–133), shortly before the architecture issue (pp. 155–206), in which Plečnik's works were published.

5. Undated letter, preserved in the architecture archives of the National Technical Museum in Prague.

6. *Volné Směry* 10 (1906), pp. 277–314.

7. The issue presents works by Kotěra: the Community Center of Hradec Králové with its staircase, the Town Hall conference room by Jindřichův Hradec, a sketch of the Landsberger burial vault, and the Kožíšek, Vojan, Maydl, Perutz, and Slukov burial vaults, as well as several funerary monuments by the architect Sucharda. Works by Josef Gočár include a burial vault and a commercial building constructed in Hradec Králové. For more information about the Art Nouveau period in Bohemia, see the exhibition catalog (produced under the direction of J. Kotalík), *Tschechische Kunst 1878–1914, auf dem Weg in die Moderne* (Darmstadt, 1984).

8. Undated letter to Jan Kotěra, preserved in the architecture archives of the National Technical Museum in Prague. Coming from Plečnik, the requirement that art be "melancholy" would not surprise Kotěra. Speaking to his students, he himself characterizes Plečnik's work as being "touched with melancholy." See J. Štěpánek, "Jože Plečnik 1872–1957," *Architektura ČSR* 16 (Prague, 1957), pp. 137–138. Elsewhere, Kotěra speaks of "the simplicity and melancholy" of Plečnik's work; *Volné Směry* 6 (1902), p. 94.

9. F. Burkhardt, M. Lamarová, *Cubismo cecoslovacco, architetture e interni* (Milan: Electa, 1982).

10. Pavel Janák replaced Plečnik both at the School of Decorative Arts (beginning in 1921) and at Prague Castle (beginning in 1936). See the exhibition catalog by O. Hertenová and V. Šlapeta, *Pavel Janák, Architektur und Kunstgewerbe* (Vienna: Semper-Depot, 1984).

11. 1916 letter to Jan Kotěra, preserved at the architecture archives of the National Technical Museum of Prague.

12. This is known through letters from Pavel Janák to Jože Plečnik, preserved at the Plečnik Museum in Ljubljana.

13. *Styl* 2 (1910), pp. 105–109.

14. *Styl* 1 (1908–9), pp. 40–49. The presentation of Wagner's "am Steinhof" church is accompanied by an article of Pavel Janák entitled "Otto Wagner."

15. Ibid., pp. 115–116. The editorial boards specifies in a note that it does not share Plečnik's point of view.

16. Ibid., pp. 129–130. This article is signed "A"; its author remains unknown. In the same issue, the same letter is used by the author of a text on the Community Center, created by Kotěra in Prostějov.

17. *Styl* 2 (1910), pp. 122–127.

18. Principally a sketch of the interior of a church (1907) reproduced in *Styl* 1 (1908–9), p. 132, and a study for the facade of the Stollwerk factory in Vienna (1910), which Oldřich Starý, in the journal *Architecktura* 4 (Prague, 1942), p. 64, says "announces, so to speak, a latter-day cubism." It is likely that Pavel Janák became aware of the design for this facade the very year of its production. A 1910 letter from Josef Gočár to Plečnik (preserved at the Plečnik Museum in Ljubljana) indicates that Janák had visited Plečnik in his Viennese studio and examined his works.

19. Letter dated September 3, 1910, to Jan Kotěra, preserved in the architecture archives of the National Technical Museum of Prague.

20. Plečnik moved into the home of Kotěra's mother, at 16 Hradešínksá Street, in the Vinohrady quarter. Kotěra lived in a villa on the same street. (Information furnished by Mirko Kotěra, son of Jan Kotěra, to whom I would like to express my thanks.)

21. In French in the original text.

22. "The works conceived during his years as a student were already distinctive due to the strong echoes of antiquity, which became accentuated and consolidated during his long sojourn in Italy. Unlike other architects, who return with boxes of meticulous sketches or with extensive knowledge about art history or with little formulas that at best allow them to produce formal shells, lacking in content, Plečnik understood *the spirit of antiquity,* appropriated it, and each of his works is now penetrated with it." J. Kotěra, "Jože Plečnik 1872–1957," *Volné Směry* 6 (1902), p. 94.

23. J. Štěpánek, "Josef Plečnik, učitel a mistr," *Architecktura* 4 (1942), pp. 57–61.

24. J. Štěpánek, "Josef Plečnik 1872–1957," *Architektura ČSR* 16 (1957), pp. 137–138.

25. Letter dated June 25, 1955 (Plečnik Museum in Ljubljana).

26. Upon the first presentation of the work of his students in the journal *Styl,* 4 (1912), pp. 176–192, Plečnik writes: "In publishing samples of the work of my students, my sole desire is to help these young people. It goes without saying that I take no personal interest in it. But for the young, such an experience is an encouragement. It doesn't matter whether it is I or another who guides these students. The teacher has but one role: to push his students to search, then to work with the idea that they will find, so that they build confidence in themselves. All the rest is superfluous. Life takes each of us into its arms of iron, pierces each of us with its thorns, and each one is— according to the decree of providence—'happy in his own way.' If I served as a guide, I did so naively, without the slightest maxim, and I will continue to do so as long as it is God's will. Another master would do differently. Nietzsche states: 'There is always something at which one is better than the other.' We say: 'Everyone knows everything,' but also: 'each one has his correct path to follow.' Thus, in the end, *vanitas vanitatum,* no one can go beyond these few square meters, and thus, we lay down to rest without vanity and we rise with modesty." A large selection of the works of his students from the Prague studio are assembled in J. Plečnik, *Výběr prací školy pro dekorativní architekturu v Praze z roku 1911–1921* (Prague, 1927).

27. Fact communicated to V. Šlapeta by Bohuslav Fuchs in Brno, July 1971.

28. Many of Plečnik's students (Josef Štěpánek, František L. Gahura, Josef Místecký, and others) continued their studies with Jan Kotěra at the Academy of Fine Arts. For a complete list of Plečnik's students, see *Architektura* 4 (1942), p. 66.

29. O. Novotný, *Jan Kotěra a jeho doba* (Prague, 1958), pp. 43–44.

30. See J. Hlavatý and Z. Kirschner, "Otto Rothmayer 28.2.1892–24.9.1966" in *Architecktura ČSR* 26 (1967), pp. 46–50.

31. Josef Fuchs (1894–1979) produced the Market Hall in Prague in collaboration with Oldřich Tyl (1924–28), the winter stadium on the Island of Štvanice, and the entry to the zoological garden in the Troja quarter of Prague. In the twenties, Ludvík Hilgert (1895–1967) built a school in Komice, Moravia, and in the thirties, many buildings in the Vsetín region, in northern Moravia, including a savings bank (1936, in collaboration with Antonín Tenzer), the Rodinger department stores (1937), and a villa in Dalečín (1936–39). Karel Řepa (1895–1963) finished his studies with Plečnik in Ljubljana; he was to be credited principally with buildings for sporting exhibitions in Pardubice (1930), the train station in Pardubice (1948–57), and the theater of Gottwaldov (1957–64, in collaboration with his son Miroslav Řepa). Josef Štěpánek (1899–1964), along with Bohuslav Fuchs, constructed an electrical center and a residential home in Háje u Mohelnice (1921–22) and a villa for the sculptor Pelikán in Olomouc (1924); he won first prize in a competition for the Parliament headquarters in the Letná quarter of Prague (1928) and the Prague-Bráník stadium (1929). At the start of the Second World War, he built a dam on the Elbe in Předměřice (1941–42).

32. František L. Gahura (1891–1958) is responsible for the planning of Zlín (today Gottwaldov), where he also built a cinema, several schools, and many types of residential homes. The most notable work of Jindřich Merganc (1889–1974) is the Koch sanatorium in Bratislava, conceived of in collaboration with Dušan Jurkovíc.

33. Alois Mezera (1889–1945), along with the architects Šrámek and Vichra, won first prize in the international competition for the Parliament in Ankara.

34. Alois Metalák (1897–c. 1983), professor at the School of Decorative Arts in Železný Brod, was one of the master designers of Czech glass.

35. Karel Štipl (1889–1972) taught decorative sculpture at the School of Decorative Arts in Prague. He designed the decorative sculpture for the Liberation Monument, situated on Vítkov hill in Prague, as well as two residential buildings in the Dejvice quarter of Prague (1933).

36. See the exhibition catalog *Bedřich Feuerstein* (Prague: S. V. U. Mánes, 1936); or the exhibition catalog *Bedřich Feuerstein 1892–1936* (Prague: S. V. U. Mánes, 1967).

37. Undated letter from Pavel Janák to Jože Plečnik for his birthday, preserved at the Plečnik Museum in Ljubljana.

38. Fact communicated to Vladimír Šlapeta by Bohuslav Fuchs in July 1971. See also Průchová Zdena, "Josef Plečnik à Praha," *Umění* 5 (Prague, 1972), p. 444.

39. In *Styl* 3, no. 8 (1922–23), p. 53.

40. See note 27. The works of Plečnik's school were also published in *Architektura* 3 (1941), p. 237. See also the article by Z. Wirth, "Dvě speciálky architecktury," *Architecktura* 3 (1941), pp. 234–236.

41. A letter from Jan Kotěra to Jože Plečnik, dated December 30, 1919 (Plečnik Museum, Ljubljana), indicates that Kotěra intended to create a new architecture studio, but was unable to find official support for this project.

42. The correspondence between Plečnik and Kotěra (preserved in the architecture archives of the National Technical Museum of Prague and at the Plečnik Museum in Ljubljana) does not enable us to determine if Plečnik refused the position or if the administration rejected his nomination. It seems the project itself came up against a lack of interest, judging from a letter that Plečnik addressed to Jan Kotěra on January 1, 1920: "The domestic scene is hardly promising. More and more vile things are happening. One senses a growing distaste for public life— a distaste one must incite people to fight against by making it clear that fleeing public life will not help change a situation; only active and resolute intervention will. Only bad principles can fail. If we must drain the cup of sorrow to the dregs, let us do so without fearing the last drops—the eye of the Lord will watch over us in the coming year, and His assistance will be refused to those inactive souls who do not solicit it."

43. See note 23.

44. In *Architektura ČSR* 7 (1948), p. 12.

45. Letter dated December 15, 1921, preserved at the architecture archives of the National Technical Museum of Prague.

46. From 1921 to 1924 Plečnik renovated President Masaryk's apartment; from 1921 to 1931, the Garden of Paradise, as well as the gardens referred to as "on the Ramparts" and "of the Bastion"; in 1922, the first courtyard with the two flagpoles. Between 1925 and 1929 he completed the stairway leading from the third courtyard to the Garden of Paradise; from 1928 to 1932, the pavement of the third courtyard with the commemorative obelisk, and from 1927 to 1929, the hypostyle entryway. See P. Janák, "Josef Plečnik v. Prazé," *Volné Směry* 26 (1928–29), pp. 97–108; R. Rouček, "Plečnikovo dílo na pražkém Hradě," *Dièlo* 34 (Prague, 1945–46), pp. 56–60; *Novosti Pražského hradu a Lán* (Prague, 1928); Z. Průchová, "Josef Plečnik à Praha," *Umĕnì* 5 (1972), pp. 442–452.

47. See note 45 and Č. Chýský, "Z presidentova bytu na Pražkém Hradě," *Byt a Umění* 1, no. 2 (Prague, 1930), pp. 1–6.

48. Among Plečnik's permanent collaborators, we can mention Otakar Hátle for metal and František Kadeřábek for stone. See note 22.

49. E. Edgar, "J. Plečnik doma," *Kámen* 22, no. 3 (Prague, 1941), pp. 35–43.

50. M. Benešová, "Rondokubismus," *Architektura ČSR* 28, no. 5 (1969), pp. 303–317.

51. V. Šlapeta, "Die tschechische Architektur der Zwischenkriegszeit," *Archithèse* 10, no. 6 (Zurich, 1980), pp. 5–19.

52. P. Janák, "Josef Plečnik v Praze," *Volné Směry* 26 (1928–29), p. 97.

53. In *Styl* 3, no. 8 (1922–23), pp. 43 and 84; and *Umění* 5 (1972), p. 445.

54. Among other things, he was elected an honorary member of the Architecture Society and of the Artistic Association of Prague. In a letter dated November 4, 1929 (preserved at the Plečnik Museum in Ljubljana), the Artistic Association again expresses its support for his work at the castle.

55. The inquiry of the Society of the Friends of Old Prague into Plečnik's projects for the northern side of the castle was published in *Za starou Prahu, věstník pro ochranu památek* 19, nos. 3–4 (Prague, 1935), pp. 17–19.

56. Ibid., p. 39.

57. Plečnik's activities at Prague Castle came to an end on November 26, 1934, with his definitive departure for Ljubljana. He nominally retained his position during the entire following year, working on a second project for the renovation of the castle's grounds. See Z. Průchová, "Josef Plečnik à Praha," *Umění* 5 (1972), p. 451.

58. See note 50.

59. Pavel Janák was named Prague Castle architect in 1936, and remained in this position until his death in 1956. Among other things, he renovated the tennis courts and the Royal Garden.

60. See note 49. In 1947, after the connection for the reconstruction of the Old City's Town Hall, Karel Řepa wrote to Plečnik in Ljubljana: "We told ourselves in Prague that only our 'old man' would be capable of working on the Old City's Town Hall." (Letter from Karel Řepa to Jože Plečnik, preserved at the Plečnik Museum in Ljubljana.)

61. This letter, preserved at the Plečnik Museum in Ljubljana, bears, among others, the signatures of Josef Gočár, Pavel Janák, Josef Chochol, Vlástislav Hofman, Otakar Novotný, Bohumír Kozák, Alois Kubíček, František Roth, Alois Dryák, Bohumil Hübschmann, Oldřich Tyl, Klement Šilinger, Alois Mezera, Jindřich Merganc, Jaroslav Vondràk, Josef Kalous, and Max Urban.

62. In the work of most of his students, Plečnik's influence can nonetheless be seen in the conception and production of details.

63. In *Kámen* 22 (1941), p. 22.

64. In *Architektura ČSR* 16 (1957), p. 137.

65. In *Architektura* 4 (1942), p. 57.

Plečnik and Czech Modernity

Alena Kubová

Guy Ballangé

The clash between architecture and culture, characteristic of Czechoslovakia at the beginning of this century, forms a backdrop against which to appreciate the contributions of those who played prominent roles in advancing the new architecture, among them Jože Plečnik. As a result of the profound transformations in Czech culture initiated by Jan Kotěra, the arrival of Plečnik, another student of Viennese fame and a Slovenian, was considered in Prague's progressive milieu to be an event of major importance. But why?

In the final years of the nineteenth century, Czech history was dominated by the political centralism of Hapsburg Vienna and by its corollary, the nationalist reaction. It was during this period that an essential shift occurred, aimed at replacing olitical projects—whose influence had been severely limited by censors—with cultural projects, which, because of their unlimited possibilities, would be difficult to contain. The problems of national identity became central to philosophical and artistic research, and the idea that a specifically Czech art had to be elaborated, distinct from European currents, finally won acceptance. Promoting the principle of national identity meant making technical and scientific progress, as well as establishing the foundation of a national culture. But while painting turned to French Impressionism, the new architecture focused on Vienna, on the school of Otto Wagner.

Keenly aware of his origins, Jan Kotěra promulgated a new concept founded on the teachings of his Viennese master. This concept, a true revolution in the nationalist intellectual milieu, would in time bring about the architectural rationalism upon which the Czech avant-garde based its theories in the early 1920s. Although largely in agreement with the principles of Otto Wagner, Kotěra's ideas were touched with a distinctly Czech flavor. We detect his interest in Czech popular art, which the nationalists perceived as traditional art. Kotěra's notion of the architectural milieu, expressed in his text of 1903, implied a new interpretation of Czech architecture. He bolstered this notion with topological, geographical, and cultural details, which allowed him to justify his rejection of the popular art "revival" espoused by traditionalists: "Taking our popular art as a basis for my analyses, I will learn about local construction techniques, about the materials that are distinctly ours, in order to create a form that will be distinctly ours."[1] In association with the undertakings of the Mánes group of artists, Jan Kotěra built, in the first years of this century, the foundations for Czech modernity.

When Jože Plečnik arrived in Prague in 1911, at stake was the will to create a new Czech architecture. The new arrival had two main references: he was a student of Otto Wagner and he was Slavic. These two references would in time increasingly contradict each other, but by recognizing the reciprocal importance of each element, the Czech vision of modernity would

be enriched. To avoid the formal distortions that nationalism could bring about, the most progressive theories concentrated on the relationship between architecture and technology. In 1903 F. X. Šalda, a friend of Kotěra and the most important critic of the time, published "The New Beauty." By insisting on the importance of technology, he defined the new aesthetic: "Technology has created a new formal language without recourse to tradition."[2] Šalda, who represented the new tendencies, as did Kotěra, specified:

Nothing is as grandiose or as impressive as the architecture of a railroad bridge, large, stripped down, without ornament, nothing but the idea of construction materialized. It is precisely on this essential clarity, this hardened purity, this honesty, and this rigidity that the aesthetic sensation close to the sense of honor and grandeur is born.[3]

In 1929 the most famous protagonist of the avant-garde Czech movement and the theoretician of constructivism, Karel Teige, wrote: "Jan Kotěra and F. X. Šalda have determined the evolutionary axis of Czech modernity."[4]

But in the beginning of the 1910s, the rationalization of architectural form was questioned by the cubists, who were aware of "the danger inherent in international and universal art resulting only from purely technological production." The cubist generation shifted the center of the architectural debate. Significantly, one of the protagonists of this trend, Josef Gočár, was a student of Kotěra, and the other, Pavel Janák, a student of Otto Wagner.

While Kotěra's rationalism functioned in the realm of conception, making style the expression of spatial organization and structure, cubism, concerned above all with formal creation, sought to function in the realm of perception. "Form is absolute and dominates utility, which generally varies according to the times," wrote V. Hofman in 1911.[5] The cubists posed the question of modernity essentially in terms of form. For Pavel Janák, "architecture is the plastic realization of an idea belonging to a period and results from stylistic thought and abstraction."[6] While pictorial cubism claimed artists such as Picasso, Braque, and Gleizes as mentors, architectural cubism adapted to the specificity of the Czech situation by referring to the theory of *Kunstwollen,* introduced by Alois Riegl.

"The year 1910 is the year the new forces arrived,"[7] proclaimed V. V. Stech, the theoretician of Czech cubism. Jože Plečnik arrived in Prague in 1911, and it was in this atmosphere of theoretical polemics that interest in him arose. His Viennese work had already been presented in *Volné Směry* and in *Styl,* the most progressive

Portrait of Plečnik by Kotěra, 1897

Easter greetings from Plečnik to Kotěra, 1913

journals of the time. It was accepted as showing proof of originality in the conscientiousness of its detail, its concern for materials, and its will to monumentalize form.

Plečnik's efforts to plant the roots of his architecture solidly in the culture and his awareness of the importance of spiritual values attracted the attention of Czech cubists. The cultural evolution attached to the notion of milieu was presented in Czech cubist theory as one of the determining factors of contemporary style: "The efforts of modern architecture must follow the general evolution, determined by laws defined in the past, as well as establish ties with the current context and needs, so that the architectural product will take into account all the determining factors of modern life."[8] Just when he was expected to take a position that would accelerate the establishment of the modernity initiated by Kotěra, Plečnik remained in the wings. In fact, he did not take part in the debate orchestrated by the cubists, who used solid theoretical arguments. Yet during this period of modernity's crystallization, one's conceptual approach counted as much as one's projects, if not more. But Plečnik remained silent when the cubists proclaimed:

By emphasizing utilitarian goals and functional efficiency, rationalism has defined an outline for architecture founded on scientific formulas, instead of defining the laws governing its conception. This means that the architecture conceived of at the time of technological discoveries has been unable to create a relationship with its milieu from a psychological point of view.[9]

For this reason, Plečnik's influence on modern architecture was limited to his teachings—important nonetheless—at the School of Decorative Arts. By not addressing the problems

posed by different theories outside of the classroom, Plečnik defined his own field of intervention and limited its effects, although his teachings, as those of Kotěra, emerged in his students' quest for liberation. The questions that would be posed created a distinction between the rationalization of the architectural conception and the creation of a beautiful form. Krejčar, a student of Kotěra, wrote in 1928, when constructivism was already established: "The beauty of the modern form corresponds to scientific and mathematical forms, it presupposes a scientific solution to the conduct of life, but cannot be attained by way of science—it is and will remain an artistic manifestation."[10]

Thus in the constitution of Czech constructivism, the role of its most visible students—J. Krejčar, F. L. Gahura, B. Feuerstein—would be to counterbalance the will of Karel Teige to place architecture in a category with science, as if, behind the concept of positivist rationalism, the need to place value on the cultural origins of architecture was taking shape among the protagonists of the Czech avant-garde, a need eminently present in Plečnik's works.

While the two schools where Plečnik and Kotěra taught were the shining lights of the new architecture, the third and the largest, the Architecture Faculty at the School for Advanced Technical Studies, lacked a new pedagogical program; the weight of academicism weighed heavily upon the experiments of its students. Updating the teaching "still dominated by the neo-Renaissance Czech style common at the time of the National Theater's construction"[11] (1883) was of primary importance after 1918. Due to its ideological nature, this reform would confirm the political and cultural dynamism of the newly created national state. Thus in November 1920 the students of the Architecture Faculty addressed a memorandum to the president of the republic, Tomáš G. Masaryk, demanding the nomination of professors representative of the new architecture, and in which reference is made to Plečnik.[12]

"In 1918, with the war ended and independence proclaimed, we thought that everything would be abandoned and that everyone would start from scratch," wrote architect Karel Honzík, one of the leaders of the avant-garde between the two world wars.[13] Art history was discarded, or at least an attempt was made to break away from the concepts of the past.

In the early twenties, the features of the avant-garde became more distinct, its point of departure marked by an aversion to the dominant teachings. For the new generation, born in about 1900, it was a matter of defining new concepts, or as the initiator of constructivism, Karel Teige, suggested, of defining "a contemporary style." This desire to "purify" architectural form, common to the first projects of the avant-garde's future members, was indicative of the desire to make a break. Only the methods of the cubist J. Chochol, undertaken in 1914, interested them, for he put into practice an idea of architectural form, designing facades composed of elementary geometric shapes and lines. In 1921 V. Obrtel, E. Linhart, K. Honzík, and J. Frágner, still students at the time, all exhibited facades composed of elementary forms.

Mere opposition to the academicism of the Faculty of Architecture, where enrollment was quasi-obligatory for first-year students, assured the ascendancy of the teachings of Plečnik and Kotěra. While the faculty was considered to be "good for preparing architectural bureaucrats or technical school teachers,"[14] the schools of fine arts and of decorative arts conserved specific values in the eyes of the young, forged by the individuality of each professor. The respect commanded by the professor helped students to measure the novelty of their projects in more subtle terms than did the simple refusal of academicism. As one writer summed up Plečnik's contribution:

While Plečnik's Viennese work may not strike us by the radicalism of its conception, its values are undeniable. J. Plečnik knew how to go beyond the guidelines of teaching, limited to exercises in ornamental composition; he transmitted two facets of his conception to his students: a sense for materials and for work well done. Even though today we may feel distant from the values extolled by Plečnik, we cannot deny the quality of his work, founded on the concern for detail and on the refinement of artisanal work.[15]

Written in 1932 on the occasion of his sixtieth birthday, this text clearly reveals the position of the Czech avant-garde with respect to Plečnik: he is honored, but for the avant-garde, preoccupied by the social role of architecture, politically and ideologically engaged in a revolutionary enterprise, the architect who was to turn Hradčany Castle into a presidential residence could not have the authority of the professor who led the way to modernity.

■ Notes

1. J. Kotěra, "O novém umění," *Volné Směry* 4 (1900), p. 192.

2. F. X. Šalda, *Volné Směry* 7 (1903), pp. 169–181.

3. Ibid.

4. K. Teige, "Vůdce české moderny," *Kmen* 12.

5. V. Hofman, "Duch moderní tvorby v architektuře," *Umělecký měsíčník* 1 (1911–12); reedited in V. Pechar, P. Uldrich, *Program České Architektury* (Prague: Odéon, 1967).

6. P. Janák, "Ve trětine cesty," *Volné Směry* 9 (1918), p. 218.

7. V. V. Stech, *Dohady a jistoty* (Prague, 1967).

8. See note 5.

9. Ibid.

10. *L'architecture contemporaine en Tchécoslovaquie* (Prague, 1928); see chapter by O. Krejčar, "L'architecture est-elle un art or une science?" (in French).

11. B. Kozak, quoted by O. Storch-Marien in his memoirs (Prague, 1966), p. 216.

12. See K. Honzík, *Ze života avantgardy* (Prague: Čs spisovatel, 1963), p. 10.

13. Ibid., p. 8.

14. See note 11.

15. "60 let J. Plečnika," *Volné Směry* 29 (1932), p. 114; article signed S. A.

WORKS

Modern or Postmodern: A Question of Ethics?

Reflections on Moral Value in the Work of Jože Plečnik

François Burkhardt

There have always been unknown artists, simply because their works did not prominently display motifs common to the dominant tendencies of their day and were therefore not associated with the history of their time. This is why many architects and their work are forgotten for many years. One such architects, whose work has recently been rediscovered, is Jože Plečnik. And yet there was no indication that he would be forgotten; indeed, two of Plečnik's constructions should have been considered the masterworks of the "modern" movement in architecture: the Zacherl house in Vienna, conceived of and constructed between 1903 and 1906, and the National University Library at the University of Ljubljana, built between 1928 and 1930. Add to that another major work, an example of the perfect integration of new architecture into a preexisting historical structure—the transformation of Prague Castle, including the planning of the surrounding courtyards and gardens, begun in 1921 and finished in 1937—and one realizes that the Viennese school, renowned modernists, never pushed the function of modern architecture so far. Such integration adds a previously unknown dimension to the Wagnerian school, an exemplary portfolio of refinement and richness of invention, already so opulent in the Viennese Secessionist school.

Another aspect that should have given Jože Plečnik his place as a master of modern architecture is his didactic work, first at the Prague School of Applied Arts, between 1911 and 1920, and then at the Architecture Faculty of his native city, Ljubljana, from 1918 until his death in 1957, where he was to train a generation of architects. He engaged them in a specifically national direction, seeking a coherent and popular language while preserving modernist, Secessionist, and classical elements.

The final point that should have made his work a lasting reference was his approach to planning, his manner of offering a reading of the city through regular interventions at strategic points, placing a series of unmistakably personal signs within an urban itinerary unique in its kind. This manner of marking a city, Ljubljana, with symbols of orientation in order to give it a historical identity, is the fruit of a type of analysis that was only later, in the sixties, to become a topic of interest thanks to Kevin Lynch and Robert Venturi: the symbolic representation of a country's architecture. The east coast of the United States was to Venturi what Slovenia was to Plečnik.

To explain the absence of Plečnik in the history of modern architecture, one must consider his work from a modernist perspective: the lack of internationalization in his language in favor of a geographically demarcated, regional approach, and the recovery of specifically local, symbolic elements that return a social and psychological dimension to architecture, a trait that was hardly appreciated by the representatives of rationalism and neopositivism who have dominated the history of modern architecture for

the past thirty years. As speculative reason took precedence over social concern, it was his antimaterialist ethic and profound religiosity that caused Plečnik to be omitted from all discussions on modernity in architecture.

This final argument will be the focus here, because it is possible to read the works and explain the methodology of Jože Plečnik only by way of his ethical approach, an approach that led him to act and express himself according to a goal defined through architecture, which was above all moral in nature.

While it is true that Plečnik's reappearance on the architecture scene is linked with the current dissension surrounding the "modern movement" and the consequences of the "postmodern" movement's appearance, this is not sufficient to explain the renewed interest of critics, who until recently focused solely on certain rationalist principles and dictated the criteria for a so-called modern architecture.

Paradoxically, it is Plečnik's ethical side that has allowed for his rehabilitation by the critics: his commitment to an architecture in which the social agenda would become a tool for emancipation. While there is basic agreement concerning the goal to be set for architecture, there is, as to the method, the result, and the function, as well as to the institutional utilization of such a political stance, complete discord.

To be more precise, Plečnik never considered the use of new technologies as a solution to any problem. This is why he was always able to combine simple, readable, modern constructions of refined elegance with regional crafts, chosen for both ethical and practical reasons, and to combine traditional methods and the

**Church of the Holy
Spirit, Vienna, 1910,
capitals in the crypt**

**Zacherl house,
Vienna, 1903–5,
detail of facade**

techniques of reinforced concrete. In 1910, for
the Church of the Holy Spirit in Vienna, for example, he used a new system of double beams
with reinforced concrete girders that stretch for
almost thirty yards without intermediary sup-
ports (a practice that was little known at the
time and that attracted the attention of the
major builders in reinforced concrete). Yet not
wanting the supporting structure to dominate,
he unhesitatingly added a series of decorative
elements, thus giving the church the intimacy
required for meditation.

Plečnik's modernism is apparent in the plan for
the support system of the Zacherl house in Vienna (1903), which clearly shows a conception
based on a square frame, to which he added

squared-off pillars at the crossing of the axes
that materialized the system and made it visible.
It is not by chance that Adolf Loos, in *Spoken in
the Void,* renders homage to Plečnik for being a
"purist" artist. The facade of the same house,
with its granite facing and inserted openings,
also demonstrates great modernity, and leads us
to wonder whether it is not Plečnik himself
who influenced Otto Wagner in his manner
of treating stone facing since this manner of
treating facades appears for the first time in
Wagner's work in 1904, on the Steinhof church.
Later on, Plečnik used systems of serial prefab-
rication for standard elements, and the refined
execution and care he brought to "modern"
details and materials shows how close he could
be to the great masters of modern architecture.
His architecture, which was rigorous, harmoni-

ous, and warm, accorded him a special position in the 1910s, falling as it did between rational rigidity and the Viennese Secessionists' decorative opulence.

He demonstrated an avant-garde attitude in the domain of interior design as well, notably in the salon of Dr. Peham in Vienna (1905), in which we sense a desire to liberate forms and allow geometric matrices to dominate. Parallel to these works, we find projects reflecting the regional Bohemian and Slovenian tradition. It seems that at all times, Plečnik amalgamated different cultures, merging them into a diversified personal interpretation that ranged from the modern to the classical.

Where Plečnik cannot be identified with the modern movement—in most of his works— is in his vision of the role of engineering and technology. While using these for precise goals, he never allowed the supporting structure to be displayed just for the pleasure of showing it off. He formed his material freely, sometimes as an architect, sometimes as a sculptor, placing great importance on expression, which, according to him, could not result from the rational application of building technologies. He placed little importance on science or on the scientific method in the evolution of construction and of building technology. Plečnik never associated with a world view according to which technology and the methods of production could

Dr. Peham's house, Vienna, 1905, salon

Weidmann house, Vienna, variation of the facade, 1902

resolve the most urgent of society's problems in terms of its need for architectonic spaces. He therefore did not identify with the avant-garde's ideas for radical transformation, based on an intellectual model of a future society. His relationship to the world of industrial production was filtered by his vision of artisanal work. On this subject, his attitude was closer to that of William Morris, who held that the faculties for cultivating the eye were closely linked to those of the hand. Like William Morris, in fact, his teaching encompassed all of the arts, with decoration playing a principal role, along with the pleasure of creating objects derived from work. It was also the component of social commitment to "handwork" and its utility that brought the two men closer together.

Plečnik was certainly in opposition to the modern movement when it sought to abolish the dimensions of history, memory, and tradition and replace them with the principle of "novelty as an absolute value." On the other hand, he shared with modernism a vision—if not a method—which sought to incorporate architecture into a collective meaning by use of the symbolism of architectural signs. Although the language of a certain "modern architecture" and Plečnik's language are different, they are united by the moral aspect of architecture with a mission. While fundamental modernism is based upon a revolutionary attitude, Plečnik sought the justification for his mission in religion and his commitment to the liberation of the Slavic minority. But for Plečnik, destiny lay in the hands of a force superior to that of men, rather than in the collective unity for which the twentieth-century avant-garde has waged its battles.

Sustained by the course of political developments after the fall of the Austro-Hungarian empire, Plečnik added patriotic reason to social concern. Contrary to the modern movement, which attempted to rise above national subdivisions to attain a universal unitarian spirit, Plečnik sought a clear distinction between cultures and ethnic groups, as did other architects in the beginning of the twenties, such as Pavel Janák, Josef Gočár, and Otakan Novotny in Bohemia, Dušan Jurkovic in Slovakia, and Techner in Hungary. These architects all came from cultures liberated from Anglo-Saxon influence; they were able to rely on a more "Mediterranean" spirit, each extracting different interpretations to accompany the popular motifs of the region he wished to revitalize. Plečnik's work bears no traces of the modern avant-garde, such as cubism, neoplasticism, or constructivism; neither futurism, expressionism, nor dada. The farther he gets from the Viennese years the less elements of a "modern" past appear in his works and the more an eclectic montage of classical elements is accentuated. We find this montage combined with pieces of a popular culture, interpreted and elegantly raised to the level of high culture, thus presenting an astonishing "free classicism," a universal grammar comprehensible to the public at large.

Postmodern criticism salvages Plečnik's work as that of a precursor to the movement. If, for historical reasons—Plečnik died almost twenty years before the definition of the postmodern movement in architecture—it is not possible to place the Slovenian master within this movement, we can easily find parallels to postmodernism in his intentions and stylistic elements. But in reality his work and his intentions prove that he is neither pre-postmodern nor modern. He is a multifaceted personality, which makes him difficult to associate with a major architectural movement; today, it is precisely this personal approach and individual interpretation that are of interest in his work. His main intention was to adapt architecture and the artistic profession in general to an ethical concept of the world, while using a diversified, pluralistic vocabulary. For him, "style" was the art of finding the means to transmit content through the best adapted forms.

Symbolism requires an abundance of identifiable elements. In this respect, Plečnik prefers richness at the cost of clarity. He does not hesitate to add decorative elements to his works, thus permitting different levels of interpretation, using a hierarchy of elements derived from the modern school or from postmodern trends. With elements "joined" to the building's structure, he founded an architecture based on a hierarchy of signs and symbols, allowing for an interpretation that is at times classical, at times regional, or even both at once. He therefore works with a value system at different levels of signification. Yet he never hides the systems cladding the supporting structure, only to display imitation rustic or pseudo-supporting elements (as do the architects of the postmodern movement), if they do not correspond to a function determined by the construction. Plečnik turns structural elements into decorative elements—a column becomes a twisted column, for example—but leaves the construction system visible. It is often the opulence of elements that distinguishes a modern minimalist structuralism from Plečnik's rational constructions. His opulence adds a decorative dimension that is not a supplementary application, but an expressive combination born of a different constructive logic. This effect is shown to advantage when, for example, an architrave beam above an entryway becomes a combined element between the facade and principal door, strongly marking the "entry" function of the building by the introduction of a variety of secondary elements. These elements form a multifunctional coherent whole, and constitute Plečnik's vocabulary.

Plečnik's concern with making architecture "obliging" is akin to the postmodern desire to take the user's needs into account; according to him, this need consists of a desire for an emotional participation that is shared equally by all. In practice, this democratic formula involves no real participation, but incorporates elements important for the well-being of the user, such as an architectural language bearing associative symbols—a "participative" practice that is also honored in postmodern architecture. Here, Plečnik uses a language derived from classical architecture in addition to traditional elements that affirm an ethnic regional identity.

This idea of democratization is exactly opposite to that of the "standard," which the functionalist architects of the 1920s adopted for the same reasons, believing they could level social differences by offering a gamut of high-quality possibilities both for the proletariat and for the upper classes—in retrospect, a utopian dream of an elite equality.

The idea of building a bridge between needs and creation while borrowing elements from classical architects is another common point between postmodernists and Plečnik. With columns, pilasters, porticos, and ornaments, we seek to evoke memory through tradition; the use of a code recognizable both by the creator and by the user permits an association with the past. The practice common to Plečnik and postmodernists consists of creating an association between what is personally experienced by the architect on the one hand and by the viewer on the other. These experiences, linked to a common history, are brought to life in architecture by the use of specific signs.

The common element of association is first the classical language, then the signs extracted from the regionalist code, which contribute to affirming the character of the place and thereby the roots of its inhabitants. Thus there can be a match between the creator's intentions and the viewer's expectations.

Like that of the postmodernists, Plečnik's architecture speaks; it serves first and foremost to communicate. Through a maximum of stimulation, through strongly expressive elements, a visually rich and communicative environment is created. To achieve this, one cannot work with simple typological or morphological structures, expecting them to fit into different settings. This is why Plečnik's works do not resemble one another, a sign of the research he put into creating structures that would affirm the identity of a site, that would mesh with local traditions and with the specific group inhabiting a geographic location, while accentuating difference through iconographic signs and not through uniformity and the reminder of an abstract, widespread typology.

Postmodernism rejects "lessons in morality," while favoring a liberal, almost libertine attitude toward composition, in which the personal satisfaction of the architect prevails. Contrary to this, Plečnik looks to morality for the criteria by which architecture must be composed and read. This reading is more than a simple semiological analysis; rather, it is a prophetic wish for a social behavior dictated by a view of the world transmitted only partially by the work. In this, Plečnik stands apart from the postmodern movement's "spectacular-commercial" vein in which forms and symbols, often without content, bear no relation to a philosophical position striving to express itself through formal expression.

In a sense, therefore, Plečnik remains modern, for the idea that a potential for progress is linked to knowledge was always his position. But in placing progress beneath the authority of a superior, religious force, which science was to eliminate through modernism, Plečnik is equally "premodern," almost gothic or baroque.

Understanding Plečnik's work today is not a matter of knowing whether he was the precursor of postmodernism or whether his attachment to the modern movement dominated his view on architecture. Anyone wishing

Žale cemetery,
Ljubljana, 1938–40,
detail of entrance to
main chapel

to explain his work must address the "driving forces" that caused him to approach architecture in a certain manner.

His first motive was *a desire to construct "a better world"* through architecture. This theme occurs repeatedly in Plečnik's statements. Ethics motivate creation. Architecture is a vehicle for a message. When Plečnik speaks of this "better world," he combines the moral with the material: inherent in the word "better" is a high-quality architecture. If architecture can bear a visible harmony, that harmony is an "inner" harmony, a spiritual force extracted from the Catholic faith. For him, only an "irreproachable" creator can assure a "perfect" architecture, in which spirituality is materialized by "purity" of expression. In order to reach this level of spirituality, he attempted to conduct himself in as exemplary a fashion as possible. He refused all payment outside of his university professor's salary and charged nothing for the work he provided the church. This explains his numerous commissions and abundant work in the domain of sacred art. Of an ascetic nature, he surrounded himself with a small number of symbolic objects, bridges between "his" world, the divinity, and himself. In this respect, his house in Ljubljana is an extremely important artifact. The use of motifs found in nature, of hieroglyphics symbolizing divinity, or the search for purity in classical beauty clearly reveal his mystical quest for a relationship between humanity and divinity as expressed by beauty, the supreme level of purity. The desire "to be human" resulted both from the religion impressed upon him by his family from childhood and from his social experience with the most underprivileged classes in Vienna. Plečnik used the church to make known what he called "Christian Socialism," a

combination of social demands and Christian ethics. The church, in his view, should be a meeting place for the community, which explains his sacred and sober body of work, his popular iconography, and ritual objects so rich in symbols.

Another moral aspect to his work is the glorification of artisanal work arising from the great personal satisfaction that the work of the craftsman, faithful companion to the architect, affords (see "Portfolio" section). "Artisanal" quality is part of the quality of Plečnik's work, which brings craftsmen into a communal effort.

His second motive was *to serve the Slovenian minority*. For Plečnik, architecture was a means to an identity. He used this tool to favor the emergence of a Slovenian nation that at the time was threatened by Austro-Germanic domination and sought to gain cultural independence. Plečnik

Church of Saint Francis of Assisi, Šiška, lamp, 1931

Prague Castle, railing, 1922

**Franciscan church,
Kamnik, Holy
Sepulcher chapel,
c. 1953**

worked against this domination, attempting to validate an architecture that would geographically mark cultural differences and define the ethnographic limits of a vital space impregnated with signs able to stimulate a highly desirable nationalist attitude in the countries of Slavic origin after the fall of the Austro-Hungarian empire. On this subject, Plečnik was in full agreement with the first Czech president, Masaryk, who entrusted him with an important national work: the transformation of Prague Castle, a prestigious site and symbol of the fight for national liberation. For this project, Plečnik mobilized all his knowledge, applying a rich, diversified language in which symbols of popular tradition delicately blend with existing architecture. His integrated technique is based on the use of regional materials along with ethnological signs, such as allegorical figures or portrayals of regional Slavic legends.

Plečnik was able to raise national decoration to the level of high culture, while in no way effacing its origins. This manner of confirming popular art was able to attain such high quality thanks to artisanal practices as refined as those of the Viennese Secessionist school. Plečnik declared his regional identity toward the end of the 1910s, citing as its origin the Julian Alps (a mountainous region in the Alpine foreland, between Trieste and Ljubljana), where he claims to have found his roots and from which he extracts the motifs we find in his constructions: the use of dry wall, the mixture of stone and brick masonry, the use of sculpted stone, the shapes of his chairs, chimney motifs, symbols marking the lintel of house entryways; or else the bas-reliefs chiseled onto exposed beams, and the decorative incrustations in plaster, at once types of graffiti and mural frieze.

Traditional Slovenian architecture

His third motive is *the use of the classical tradition*. Plečnik's relationship to classical art and styles is typically Mediterranean. He preferred Greek or Roman art to Anglo-Saxon neoclassical styles, but especially admired Etruscan art, which he knew in detail. He freed himself from all dogmatic canons, thus opening his work to experimentation and the invention of variations on the theme of classical Mediterranean architecture. His idea was to use the classical repertoire freely, in very personal montages. He demonstrated that the classical language could be incomplete, modifiable, as was seen in Italy in the 1950s in the neoliberty and neobaroque styles.

Plečnik's struggle against modernism is a struggle for the user's access to architectural language, but especially for the spectator's access through assimilation of a refined code that would allow for identification. In his view, to better manifest one's patriotic and democratic desires, one must take a different route than that of the avant-garde, which cut its ties with the masses. Already in 1902, Plečnik wrote, "Like a spider, I aim to attach a thread to tradition, and beginning with that, to weave my own web"—a web composed of elements drawn from among the tendencies of his time. We have here a good definition of the individual work of a noble loner, marked by a mixture of patriotic, aristocratic, and Christian sentiments, available to those who asked for his services: above all, political authorities and the institutions and representatives of the Catholic clergy.

It is difficult to demand an ethical mission from today's architecture because of the changes that have taken place in the past few decades concerning the role of architecture in society. Plečnik could still count on shared tastes and goals, and he put into practice a world view that is difficult to comprehend today. Along with the desire for an emancipating universality, the idea of progress—in the moral sense—through architecture has disappeared. Deprived of this ethical mission, the dialogue surrounding architecture concentrates on problems of technological and stylistic adaptation, characteristic of the current postmodern movement.

In the end we are faced with an individual who was able to stand by his choices and who, without making compromises, was able to define his style according to a personal vision of content, to which he remained dedicated in his work. The absence of an ethical agenda renders architecture's message frivolous and superficial. This is why Plečnik's message continues to be of interest and importance.

PORTFOLIO

Jože Plečnik in 1926

Competition project
for the Zacherl house,
Vienna, 1900

Zacherl house, details
of facade, 1904

Sketch, 1904

Sketch for house,
detail, 1906

**Zacherl house,
Vienna, 1903–5**

Zacherl house

**Zacherl house,
sketch of detail, 1904**

**Zacherl house,
sketch of detail, 1904**

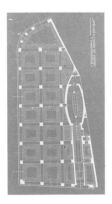

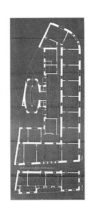

**Zacherl house,
plan of ground floor**

Plan of first floor

**Zacherl house,
stairway**

Church of the Holy
Spirit, Vienna, 1910–13,
principal facade

Church of the Holy
Spirit, variation, 1910

Church of the Holy Spirit, design for nave, 1910

Nave, 1913

Church of the Holy Spirit, the crypt under construction, 1910

Sketches for a church facade, 1902

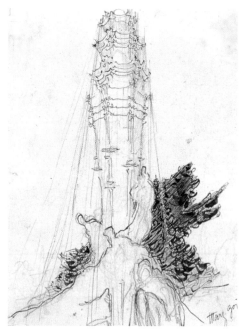

Belvedere, 1898   **Balustrade pylon,** 1900   **Monument,** 1901

Facade, 1901

Pedestal for a vase,
c. 1898

Pylon and balustrade,
1901

Monument, 1901

Chapel, 1901

Ornament, 1901

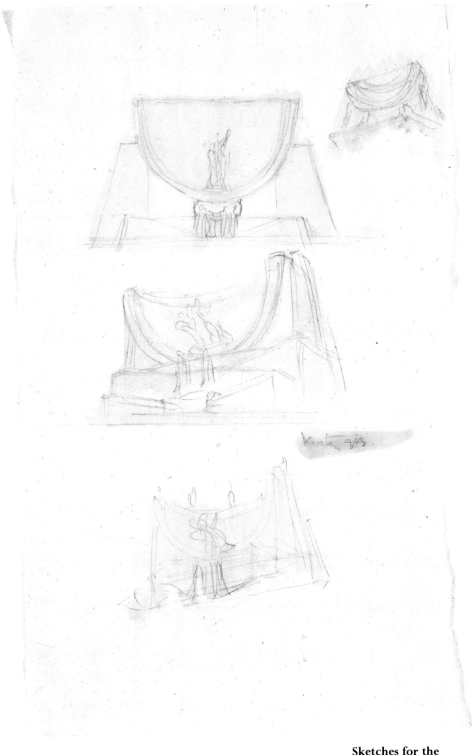

Sketches for the
competition for the
monument to Jan
Žižka, Prague, 1912

**Chalice for Andrej
Plečnik, 1913**

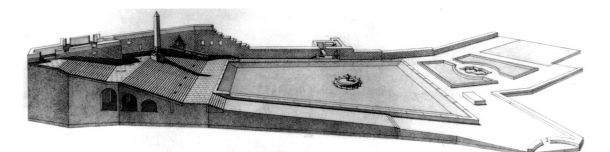

**Prague Castle, design
for the Garden of
Paradise, 1921**

**Prague Castle, third
courtyard, 1928–32**

Prague Castle, design
for a large staircase
and for the monument
to Czech soldiers, 1923

Prague Castle,
monolithic basin,
c. 1924

**Prague Castle,
stairway between the
third courtyard and
the garden, 1927–31**

**Prague Castle, Plečnik
Room, 1926–28**

**Prague Castle,
passage beneath the
main stairway, 1924**

Diorite vase, c. 1927

**Canopy stairway,
1930–31**

**The small belvedere,
1927**

Prague Castle,
entrance to the
Garden of Paradise,
c. 1924

Prague Castle,
Plečnik Bridge near
Powder Gate, 1931–32

Prague Castle,
stairway leading from
the third courtyard to
the garden, 1927–31

**Prague Castle,
aviary, 1924**

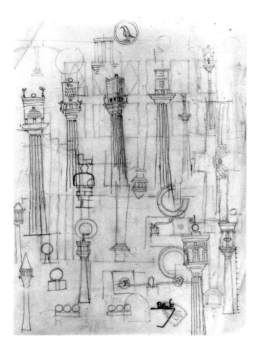

**Prague Castle, studies
for the monument to
Czech soldiers, 1923**

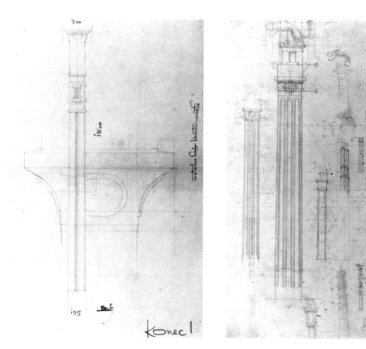

**Prague Castle, view
of the first courtyard
with one of the two
flagpoles, 1922–23**

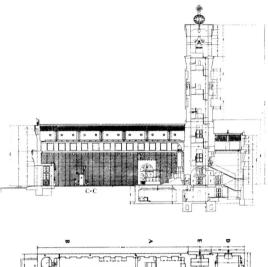

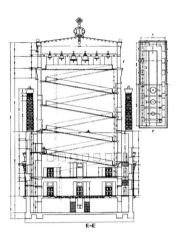

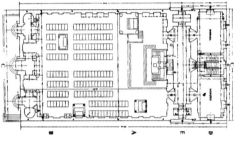

**Project for the
Sacred Heart Church,
Prague, 1927**

**Sacred Heart Church,
1928–33, view of the
parvis**

**Sacred Heart Church,
nave, 1928–32**

**Sacred Heart Church,
crypt, 1932–33**

**Sacred Heart Church,
side wall**

**Sacred Heart Church,
ramp inside the bell
tower**

Church of Saint
Francis of Assisi,
Šiška, Ljubljana,
1925–31, bell tower

Church of Saint
Francis of Assisi, nave

Church of the Virgin
of Lourdes, Zagreb,
crypt, 1936–37

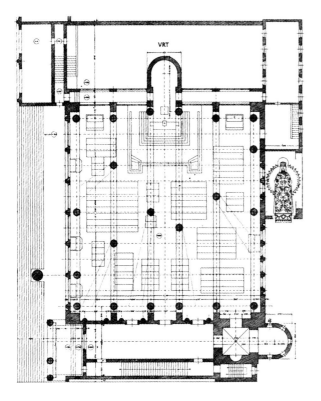

VRT

Church of the Virgin
of Lourdes, Zagreb,
plan, 1934

Church of the Ascension, Bogojina, 1925–27

Church of the Ascension

**Church of the
Ascension, interior**

Saint Michael Church,
Barje, Ljubljana,
1937–38, porch

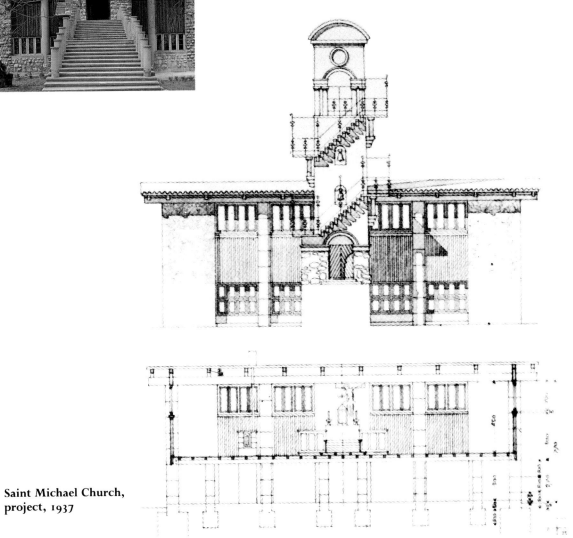

Saint Michael Church,
project, 1937

Saint Michael Church,
interior

Saint Michael Church,
detail of interior

Staircase in the
Chamber of Commerce,
Craft, and Industry,
Ljubljana, 1925–27

**Staircase in the
Chamber of Commerce,
Craft, and Industry**

**Headquarters of the
Vzajemna Insurance
Company, Ljubljana,
1928–30**

Detail of facade

**Headquarters of the
Vzajemna Insurance
Company**

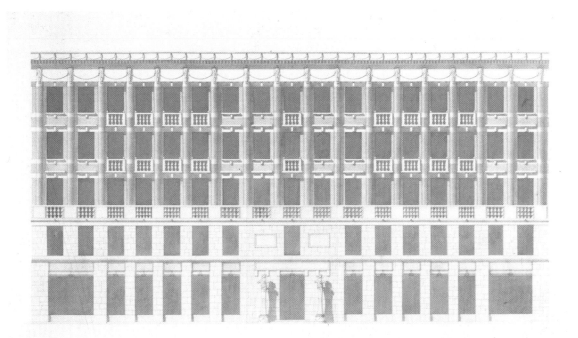

**Headquarters of the
Vzajemna Insurance
Company, elevation**

Headquarters of the
Vzajemna Insurance
Company, principal
staircase

First-floor room

Principal staircase

Vestibule

Headquarters of the Vzajemna Insurance Company, courtyard facade

Small staircase

National University
Library, Ljubljana,
east facade, 1936–41

**National University
Library, staircase**

National University
Library, Reading
Room

Reading Room

Entrance

**Door to the
Exhibition Room**

Prelovšek house,
Ljubljana, 1932–33,
salon

Prelovšek house:

Library

Salon chair

Votive lamp

Ciborium

Tabernacle

Cork

Ashtray

Cork

Doorknob

**Works executed
between the late
1930s and the 1950s**

Doorknob

Chandelier

City of the Dead, Žale
cemetery, Ljubljana,
1938–40, entrance

City of the Dead, Žale
cemetery, main chapel

**City of the Dead,
Žale cemetery,
detail of main chapel**

Žale cemetery,
workshop for coffins

Details of facade

**Žale cemetery,
Saint John Chapel**

Columns, Walls, Space

Boris Podrecca

In contemplating the work of Jože Plečnik, one is tempted to agree with Davilers when he says that "the origins of the architectural orders must be almost as ancient as humanity itself."

This observation, which implies the temporality of architecture, leads us to approach Plečnik historically. The *parlante* of his columns, walls, and spaces runs like a leitmotif throughout his work. And this is true both for the *forma mentis* and for its subjective interiority, its moods. Plečnik's classicism—and his grammar can be termed classical—is fundamentally different from one that places a conceptual super-structure on a construction or one that imposes an ideology on it. His columns are not products of a "rule book." The *parlante* of a capital, aside from the hierarchy or the dignity it implies, is in the end but the purification of the act of building itself, which is why the architecture of his columns is of archaic and epic origins, and their arrangements a dispute with history. We know that Michelangelo, using the columns of Vitruvius, relegated the latter to second-rate status, even calling him *cattivo guidizio.*

Plečnik's language also contains the drama of the transgression and reconstruction of dogma. But a rupture with history cannot rid a capital of its meaning or suppress it, prodded though we may be by the urgency of new modes of living. Plečnik see no "logical" rapport between the goals of the modern movement and the world. Through his columns, rather, he seeks the coexistence of the old with the new, to add meaning to this world.

If we abandon the positivist and linear interpretation of architecture for a moment, we might say that creating, stratifying, and thereby preserving the elements of history is just the opposite of introducing a return to the past. Instead it is the integration of history into the present; history becomes a historical form— as Loos said of his column at the Chicago Tribune—about which we can, we must, even, all agree.

Confronting and disputing history does not mean rejecting its rules or inventing a new language. This is why Plečnik believed one could make use of "eternal" means, leaving them intact and integrating them into a new, temporal context. The choice of elements itself is already foreseen in the historical authenticity of the *being-there,* and thus already made. "The forms are *there,* forms of life, old and new; starting, stopping, they live on, expressing the essence of the situation, silently expressing what no one agrees upon with words or concepts," says Wittgenstein.

Plečnik believes that the conditions for history reside only in the present; but only through history can they be divided into themes. Architecture must first, claims Loos, awaken sentiments. It follows that the classicism of the column in Plečnik's work expresses, with its Doric, Ionic, Corinthian, Athenian, Aeolian, Tuscan, composite and flowering capitals, right down to the tree trunk of Delorme, the duration and breadth of the temporality of *our own* history.

The stone Aeolian-Ionic column of the National University Library, the curved Doric colonnade at the market and the "Mycenian" columns set into the wall of the Vzajemna Insurance Company Building—all in Ljubljana—are "possibilities" of classicism as well as its transgression in our historical context. The capital of the library is not only a formal reference or citation. Its bronze Ionic scrolls, affixed to the stone, refer to a theoretical approach that relegates the use of metal to a secondary decorative role. This was the approach of Semper or of Schinkel, according to whom metal is an "unpoetic" material, as it was originally only a liquid, which we therefore do not have the right to incorporate into a primary ossature. Yet the hint of the Ionic style in this column reminds us of the symbolic approach to cultural monuments: the order was recommended by Serlio and Sandart for *uomini litterati.* Sturm also suggests that the Ionic should adorn public buildings, and Fischer von Erlach used it as a supporting order for the library of the Vienna court.

We might even think that Fisher's "historical architecture"—in which the pluralistic utilization of historical materials is legitimated right down to the "Capriccio"—and the pluralism of Semper's "experiments" were the forerunners of stratification in Plečnik's use of history. The idea for introducing this interplay into his language takes root beginning in 1910, following the model of the Beuron School's paleo-Christian ideal, Ruskin's "seven flames," and Morris's socialist program. This leads principally to the classical tension of columns and to the abandonment both of Secessionist lasciviousness and of the Viennese intellectual pomp found in

a Semper or a Wagner. Yet, despite it all, in the materiality and treatment of Plečnik's construction, we find the echo and the metaphor of the origin of all forms acquired during his apprenticeship in Vienna, independent of his will or of his explicit message.

The Semper trilogy, floor-wall-ceiling, the textile-like genesis of architecture, the "dressing," the ceramic, the tectonic, and the stereotomic run throughout the Mediterranean character of Plečnik's work. The progression of his language, its synthesis and self-examination, are best seen at the cemetery of Žale: a veritable city of the dead. From the sparsely colored main entrance, with its "useless" Roman columns, to the typological and chromatic history of the chapel of the dead, to the textured workshop—multicolored because it is part of "this world"—Plečnik acts out the eternal conflict between column and wall, between floor and ceiling, between space and its envelope. The varied treatment of the walls, their haptic, ornate appearance, the general *parlante* of their surfaces are, in the Semperian sense, the final metaphors for the antique idea of finish in the development of an architectural order. It is an organization that in principle relies on the spiritual. And it is here that the "purifying" technique in the tragic epic of Plečnik's architecture is different from the scientific positivism of Semper or Wagner.

The disputes between the Settocento and the Ottocento as to monochrome and polychrome, and over "Phidias white" and the colored incrustation of resuscitated antiquity, are synthesized in an ambivalent manner in Plečnik's treatment of walls. Both Polygnote's oligochrome and Pausanias's polychrome are equal "possibilities" for a wall's dressing. But they do not appear as simple, formal illustrations;

rather, decoration is tied in with the conditions of the space. Thus, the concept of *usus,* of utilization, appears in Plečnik's work as a secondary characteristic, not as a language in itself.

The concrete ossature, the prefabricated cement window, the pipe used as a column, the "dignified" adaptation of profane objects, the playing with materials, all constitute the "possibilities" of an architecture tied in with an "empirical artistic doctrine," but which must be subordinate to a higher symbolic order. Here it becomes visible that the archaeology of knowledge in Plečnik's works, as far as typology and space are concerned, does not open onto a universal reality. It is not the "tranquility" of a Durand that runs through the decomposition and reunification of history. Not only is history hermeneutic, but architecture cannot, according to Plečnik, simply objectify reality.

Sphere, cone, pyramid, circle, and elliptical forms intertwine in the search for a new world order. In this prodigious process, the resistance of form and of space, their origins and limits, are clearly put to the test.

The myth of community stretches across Plečnik's art of construction, but without criticism of what exists and without any radical and visible modifications. The work's aura is of primary importance, the condition and the fiction of a "metahistoric" dimension of man. His columns, walls, and space, included in the parsimonious abstinence of his life, are in the end "inventions" of his history as a secular dimension and as a contradiction to the present.

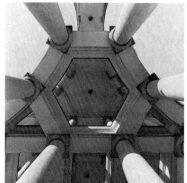

**Prague Castle,
stairway, President
Masaryk's apartments,
1922**

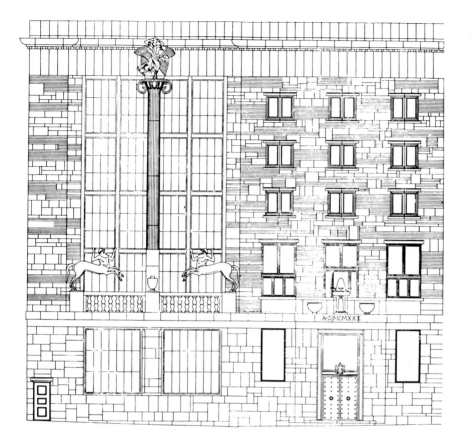

National University Library, Ljubljana, 1936, facade

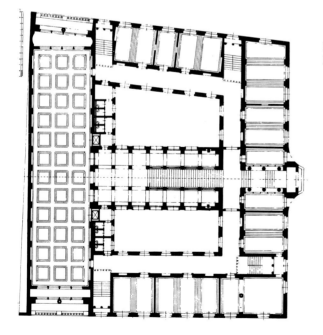

National University Library, plan

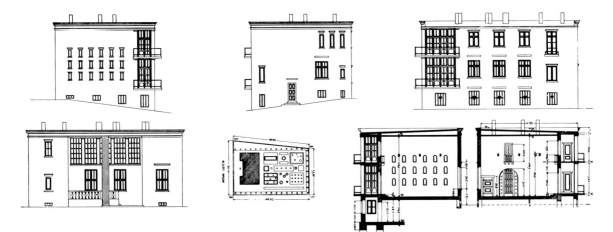

**Project for a house,
Belgrade, 1936**

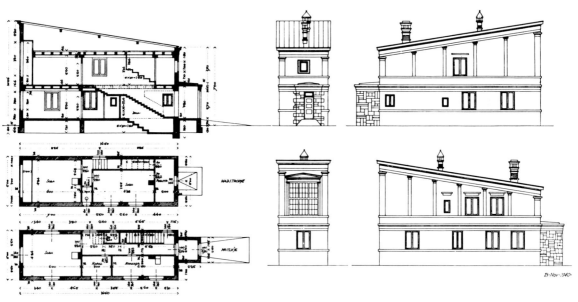

**Project for a house,
Ljubljana, 1940**

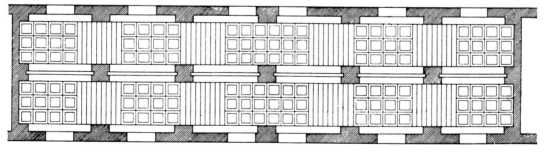

**Project for a staircase,
Ljubljana Castle, c. 1946**

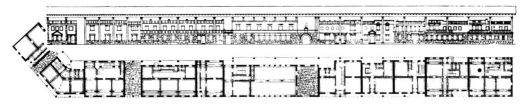

1:2000

Project for a "House under a Municipal Roof," Ljubljana, 1944

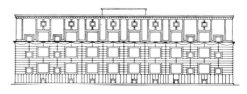

M 1:200

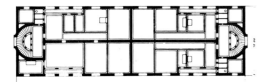

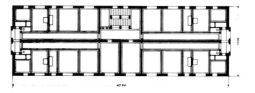

Project for an apartment building, Ljubljana, 1938

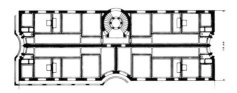

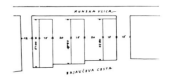

**Project for the City
Hall, Ljubljana, 1941**

**Ursulines High
School, Ljubljana,
1941**

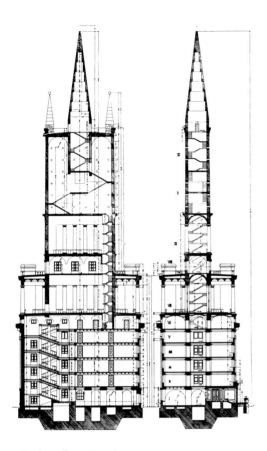

Project for a Jesuit
"monastery-bell tower,"
Osijek, 1944

Project for a
monastery and Holy
Cross Church, Zagreb,
c. 1947

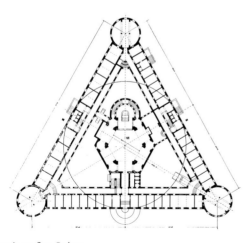

Project for Saint
Mary of the Angels
Seminary, Sarajevo,
1939

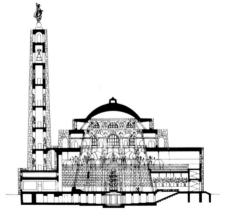

Project for Saint
Anthony Church,
Dolina, near Bosanska
Gradiska, 1948

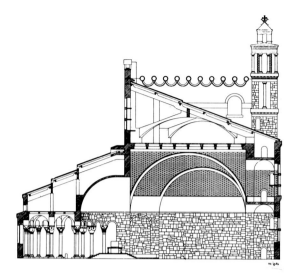

**Project for the
restoration of Maria
Bistrička Church,
1943, cross section**

Plan

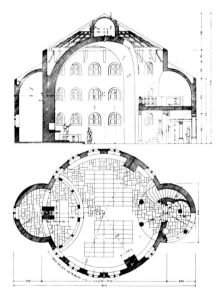

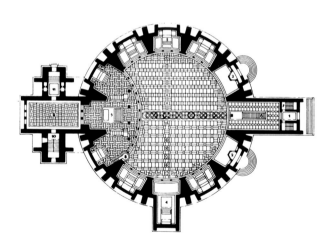

**Project for Saint
Joseph Cathedral,
Sarajevo, 1935,
cross section**

Plan

**Project for a Slovenian
Parliament, Ljubljana,
1947, cross section**

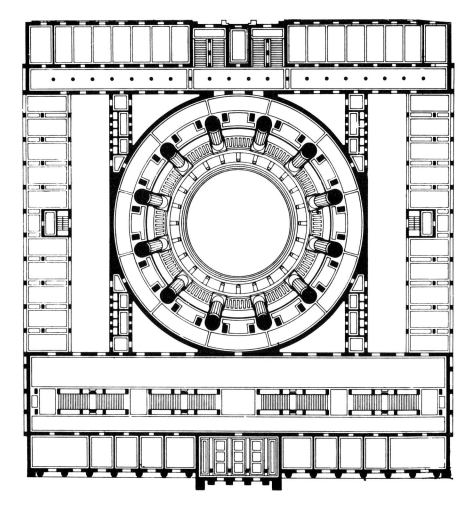

**Project for a Slovenian
Parliament, plan**

A City Promenade

Lucius Burckhardt

Linde Burkhardt

To understand the dynamics of Jože Plečnik's architecture, it suffices to follow him through Ljubljana on one of the promenades he created. The ascent to the castle seems exemplary from this perspective: any child, even the child hiding in all of us, is tempted to scale the rocks over-looking the city in order to reach the castle. Yet aside from its magnificent views, Ljubljana Castle is not a spectacular monument; it almost seems as if Plečnik's promenade does not follow the tiresome path leading directly from the old city to the castle. It follows the river for a short distance, then winds around the castle's hill, so that the visitor reaches the summit by a pleas-ant curve and arrives from the rear. The stroller then discovers the "castle" (the ramparts) without noticing right away that it is one of Plečnik's creations. Yet we cannot compare Plečnik's false castle to the false ruins of an English garden; it is not merely an eye-catching construction. In passing through it we discover many architectural elements that are interesting in their own right.

Plečnik's guided visit therefore leads us from the rear of the hill toward the notched wall we see at an angle. On the left side, facing south, in a semicircular window that has been cut into the wall, the approaching visitor sees people whom he supposes to be inside the building. Encouraged by the prospect of entering the building himself, he turns to the right toward the castle's entrance, discovering other openings from which other visitors admire the panoramic view. The approaching visitor then crosses the threshold to arrive inside the castle. But to his great surprise, after climbing a staircase and passing through the door, he finds himself not inside, but outside once again. The steps continue the length of the wall, leading the stroller to an opening through which he can enjoy the view. He approaches the window, at this point realizing that he in turn has become one of the visitors whom he had just seen from below. The château has neither interior nor exterior, it is merely an L-shaped wall, which, from one side as from the other, gives the illusion that an interior is to be found on the other side. Continuing his climb a bit farther, the visitor has the choice of leaving the castle through the semicircular door seen from below or of following the battlements of the L-shaped wall. The two itineraries lead to a circular intersection right where the visitor originally thought the castle to be, then to a path leading around the real castle, the panoramic lookouts, and to the land descending to the old city.

We can learn several lessons from this promenade. It teaches us that a promenade is not a dull path we follow in one direction and back to reach a place of interest, but rather functions on the principle of a strand of pearls: points of great interest alternate with less attractive ones. The succession of points must be conceived in such a way that the closer, intermediary points incite one to continue, so that in the end one has the memory of an interesting itinerary. This

idea of planning urban promenades, moreover, was used by the Scottish city planner Sir Patrick Geddes for the city of Dunfermline.

Used in this manner. the promenade is a unique setting in which one's senses become integrated. Although the images present themselves successively and in a fragmentary fashion, in the end the stroller has a global image of the zone upon which to create his own impressions. There is no need for any one place to characterize the region or the city; it is the promenade in its entirety that gives us the impression of an urban landscape or environment. Plečnik made use of this phenomenon to realize his most treasured goal.

Plečnik's intentions in Ljubljana were both political and religious. He wanted to create the secret capital of Slovenia, a Catholic nation. But the situation being what it was, he had neither the possibility nor, most likely, the desire to create a new capital constructed around ideal images. He preferred to deal with the city as it was, to present it as a capital in its current state. Plečnik was too subtle to erect monumental constructions, like the Victor-Emmanuel monument in Rome: Ljubljana was to give the impression of being a capital only in a fragmentary fashion, in the manner of the promenade. Plečnik's urban architecture is not monumental, but dynamic.

Upon strolling in Ljubljana, one quickly discovers the roads to which Plečnik lent a dynamic character: we feel the best example of this is the street alongside the Roman wall. Archaeological elements are integrated within a series of

In climbing the hill . . .

. . . we discover the "castle";

from inside, visitors look upon . . .

. . . those seeking an entrance.

The interior of the "castle" . . .   . . . is yet another exterior;

the path leads to the belvedere . . .   . . . from which we were observed.

The Roman wall seen from the street . . .

. . . is a passageway to the park . . .

. . . wall? romantic ruin?

From the monument to Gregočič . . .

. . . strollers can choose . . .

. . . between a raised walkway . . .

. . . and a ground-level passage.

We discover a pyramid.

fictitious monuments, pyramids, and cupolas, which upon closer inspection reveal themselves to be small doors leading to steps. In passing through these doors, the pedestrian leaves the sidewalk bordering the street to find himself on the other side of the Roman wall, where he reaches a narrow pedestrian path parallel to the street, a kind of Via Appia. The two pedestrian walkways—the regular sidewalk and the path on the other side of the wall—afford different perspectives on the urban environment. When seen from the street, the Roman wall appears severe, almost intact, and completed by new construction; while seen from he other side it appears to be in ruins, buried in vegetation, with the modern constructions far in the distance.

French Revolution Square offers another example. The stroller can actually choose among three itineraries alongside the library and the music academy: the normal sidewalk; a lane on the ramparts lined with benches and plants that invites one to rest a moment and leads, by way of footbridges, to the elevated ground floor of the neighboring buildings; or else a "delivery path" along the length of the houses that reveals their basements. This double pedestrian lane effect is used in a third manner between the pyramid and the garden of the German chevaliers.

The promenades that were planned and, in part, realized by Plečnik in the western part of town, through the "cultural quarter" in the direction of Tivoli park, and toward the north

in the direction of the Žale cemetery, can no longer be completed today because of changes made in the routing of traffic. But the great didactic itinerary the length of the Ljubljanica has remained intact. Upstream, the promenade begins—or ends—at the electrical center: a raised garden with benches in the shade of the trees allows one to follow the process by which the tumultuous waters of the stream are tamed to produce energy. The building's Egyptian disguise is reminiscent of the castle-shaped structures at the outlet of Roman aqueducts before the water is distributed and at the entrance to the salt works of Chaux.

Following the waterway, the stroller watches as it is tamed and transformed from a mountain stream to an urban stream. The banks are steeper and higher up; toward the end, the river runs between the walls; banks, bridges, streets, and buildings form a single whole. The visitor can then choose to follow the river at several levels. The culminating point of this exhibition is reached at the Three Bridges: these serve not only as river crossings, but also provide access to a lower level, closer to the water. The effect is diminished before the bridges by the covered market; it is prolonged a moment on top of the bridge, and emphasized even more on the right bank by monumental steps that cut into the upper street level behind the first row of houses.

At the two subsequent bridges, the banks, steep like those of a canal, define two spaces along the river, the limits of which are emphasized by an ensemble of balustrades, columns, and street lamps. Downstream from the last bridge, the stroller catches an early glimpse of what he

The promenade along the Ljubljanica . . .

... begins at the lock;

the river is channeled ...

... and flows under the Three Bridges ...

... then under the Shoemaker's Bridge.

Quays aid the passage . . .   **. . . from the city to the country.**

A small tributary . . .   **. . . offers a different promenade . . .**

... that passes over Trnovo Bridge ...

... and continues along a row of birch trees.

would normally see much farther along, the passage from the city to the country and the point at which the river, until then narrowly confined, is set free. The spot is marked on the right bank by the junction with a small, spectacularly landscaped river, where a strip of land that juts out causes the formation of foaming whirlpools. From that point on, downstream, the banks of the Ljubljanica have been leveled. The stroller can approach the water and sit on the banks, while admiring the great willows that adorn them.

But he can also move away from the principal body of water and follow the small tributary, the junction of which has been arranged in an equally grandiose fashion. Its banks also received architectonic restructuring; alongside the principal route is a path for more leisurely strollers. Between the bridges, the path descends to the water's edge, and the descent and ascent each afford glimpses of a striking little area originally intended for washing clothes. The attentive stroller may observe a change in the nature of the trees: the willows become rarer, the birches more numerous. The promenade ends at Emonda Bridge, which, aside from its pyramids and obelisks, seems to present no special characteristics—until one suddenly realizes that the bridge is the continuation of a birch-lined street that runs from downtown to a neighborhood church. The line of birches continues uninterrupted, and the stroller cannot help but wonder how trees can grow on a bridge.

Here again, as in the case of the illusory castle, it seems that Plečnik is giving us a friendly lesson in city planning: he did not intend to create what is generally called an urban landscape in

Ljubljana, a landscape that could easily be captured in a picture postcard, in the style of the Ponte Vecchio, the Piazzetta, Ile Saint-Louis, or Tower Bridge. Rather his objective was to allow the faculties of perception and the visual memory of the city dweller or the stroller to progressively and constantly forge their own urban vision of Ljubljana.

APPENDIXES

Chronology

1872
Born January 23, in Ljubljana into a family of woodworkers. Learns woodworking in the family business.

Educated at School of Applied Arts in Graz, where he has his first contact with architecture

1889
In Vienna begins work as a designer for a furniture manufacturer

1894
Works in Otto Wagner's studio

1895–98
Studies with Otto Wagner at the Academy of Fine Arts in Vienna

1898
Receives a degree in architecture; wins Prix de Rome; travels in Italy and France

1900
Works in Otto Wagner's studio

1901–11
Establishes his own architecture firm in Vienna

1912
Recommended by the faculty council of the Academy of Fine Arts in Vienna to succeed Otto Wagner

1911–21
Professor at the School of Applied Arts in Prague

1921–56
Professor at the Polytechnical School of Ljubljana

1921–35
Restoration of Prague Castle for the President of the Czech Republic, T. G. Masaryk

1922
Returns to Ljubljana

1952
Doctor Honoris Causa at the Polytechnical School of Vienna and at the University of Ljubljana

1957
Dies in Ljubljana

Principal Projects

Vienna Period

The Langer house and Langer building, 1900–2

The Loos house, Melk, 1901

The Zacherl house, 1903–5

Karl Borromaüs fountain, 1906–9

Church of the Holy Spirit, 1910–13

The Zacherl house, Döbling, 1909–12

Prague Period

Restoration of Prague Castle (apartments, courtyards, gardens), 1921–35

Restoration of the summer residence of the president of the Czech republic, T. G. Masaryk, Lány, 1921–23

Sacred Heart Church, 1928–32

Slovenian Period

Restoration of the Chamber of Commerce, 1925–27

Restoration of the Church of the Ascension, Bogojina, 1925–27

Church of Saint Francis of Assisi, Šiška, 1925–27

Vzajemna Insurance Company Building, 1928–30

Church of Saint Anthony of Padua, Belgrade, 1929–32

Restoration of the banks of the Ljubljanica, 1930–39

Trnovo Bridge and restoration of the banks of the Gradaščica, in the early 1930s

National University Library, 1936–41

Saint Michael Church, Barje, 1937–38

Žale Cemetery, 1938–40

Saint Benedict Church, Stranje, 1946–50

Project for the Slovenian Parliament, 1947

Brioni Pavilion for President Tito, 1956

Selected Bibliography

Kosta Stranjnić. *Josip Plečnik*. Zagreb: Čelap i Popovac, 1920.

"Práce prof. Plečnika z let 1901–1922." *Styl* 7, no. 3 (1922–23). The works of Professor Plečnik from 1901 to 1922.

Novosti pražského hradu a Lán. Prague, 1928. Reproductions of works without texts.

[J. Plečnik]. *Projekt chrámu Srdce Ježíšova na Král. Vinohradech*. Prague, 1928.

F. Stelè. *Jože Plečnik na Hradčanih in v Ljubljani*. Ljubljana, 1930. Taken from *Dom in sveta*, 1929.

J. Plečnik, F. Stelè. *Projekt univerzitetne bibiloteke v Ljubljani*. Ljubljana, 1933. Project for the University Library in Ljubljana.

[J. Plečnik]. *Studija franjevačkoga hrama Majke Božje Lurdske u Zagrebu*. Ljubljana, 1935. Study for Our Lady of Lourdske Church in Ljubljana.

[J. Plečnik]. *Aedes sancti Josephi Patriarchae*. Ljubljana, 1935.

F. Stelè, A. Trstenjak, J. Plečnik. *Architecture perennis*. Ljubljana: Mestna občiina Ljubljanska, 1941. Drawings, plans, and reproductions of works by Plečnik.

F. Stelè. "Plečnik Jože." *Slovenski biografski leksikon*. Ljubljana: Slovenska akademija znanosti in umetnosti, 1949. Includes a bibliography.

F. Stelè, J. Plečnik. *Napori*. Ljubljana: Slovensak akademija znanosti in umetnosti, 1955. Sequel to *Architecturae perennis* with drawings, plans, and reproductions of the works of Plečnik and his students.

F. Stelè, "Jože Plečnik." *Letopis Slovenske akademije znanosti in umetnosti* VIII, Ljubljana, 1958, pp. 61–76.

F. Stelè. "Od obliča do velemojstra." *Koledar družbe sv. Mohorja za leto 1958* (almanac of the Sv. Mohorja Association, 1958), pp. 46–62.

M. Mušič. *Architecktura in čas*. Maribor: Obzorja, 1963. Excerpts from articles on his friendship with the sculptor Meštrović and the architect Kotěra.

B. Podreka. *Josef Plečnik 1872–1957*. Vienna, 1967. Collection of documents from the first Plečnik exhibition.

F. Stelè. *Arh. Jože Plečnik v Italiji 1898–1899*. Ljubljana: Slovenska Matica, 1967. Letters and notes by the architect during his travels in Italy.

D. Grabrijan. *Plečnik in njegova šola*. Maribor: Obzorja, 1968. Articles and documents on Plečnik and his school.

M. Pozzetto. *Jože Plečnik e la scuola di Otto Wagner*. Turin: Alba, 1968.

[L. Gostiša]. *Arhitekt Jože Plečnik*. Ljubljana, 1968. Catalog of the Plečnik exhibition in Ljubljana, with an excerpt from Stelè's 1958 article and a complete bibliography.

M. Mušič. "Plečnik in Beograd." *Zbornik za likovne umetnosti*. Novi Sad: Matica srpska, 1970, 1971, 1973. Collection of three articles on Plečnik and Belgrade.

Z. Průchova. "Josef Plečnik à Praha." *Umeni* XX (1972), pp. 442–452.

J. Omahen. *Izpoved*. Ljubljana: Cankarjeva Založba, 1976. Memories of Plečnik and of his school.

D. Prelovšek. *Josef Plečnik. Wiener Arbeiten 1896 bis 1914*. Vienna: Tusch, 1979.

M. Pozzetto. *La scuola di Wagner 1897–1912*. Trieste: Comune di Trieste, 1979. German edition, Vienna and Munich: Schroll, 1980.

[B. Podrecca]. *Josef Plečnik. Seminar in Laibach*. Munich, 1980. Photocopy of the study done at the Superior Technical School in Munich on Plečnik's workshop.

R. Bassett. "Ljubljana 1925." *Architectural Review* 168, no. 1004 (1980). Article on the former Chamber of Commerce.

R. Bassett. "Plečnik in Ljubljana." *Architectural Review* 170, no. 1014 (1981).

M. Mušič. *Jože Plečnik.* Ljubljana: Partizanska Knjiga, 1980. The second monograph on Plečnik following the work by Stragnić.

B. Podrecca. "Jože Plečnik." *Casabella* 46 (1982), pp. 476–477.

Arhitektov bilten 62–63 (Ljubljana, 1982). Issue devoted to Plečnik. Italian edition, *Il Ritorno del mito,* Venice, 1983.

Urbanistični načrti za Ljubljano Jožeta Plečnika. Ljubljana: Arhitekturni Muzej, 1982. Catalog from the exhibition of Plečnik's designs for Ljubljana, from the architect's archives.

Jože Plečnik 1872–1957. Architecture and the City. Oxford, 1983. Publication accompanying Plečnik exhibitions in Oxford and London.

[N. Schuster]. *Josef Plečnik. Hradschin-Prag.* Munich, 1983. Photocopy of a study done in Munich—at the Superior Technical School—on Plečnik's additions to Prague Castle.

M. Pozzetto. "Žale: Obitorio giardino." *Lotus International* 38 (1983).

G. C. Leoncilli Massi. "L'autoinganno. Il caso Jože Plečnik." *Gran Bazaar* (November 1983).

Sinteza 65–68 (Ljubljana, 1984). Notes from a symposium on Plečnik.

D. Prelovšek. *Hisa slovenske zavarovalnice.* Ljubljana: Zavarovalna Skupnost Triglav, 1985. Monograph on the Vzajemna Insurance Company Building. English edition, *Slovene Insurance Company Building,* Ljubljana, 1985.

A. Suhadolc. *Plečnik in jaz.* Trieste: Založnistvo Tržaskega tiska, 1985. Letters from J. Plečnik to Anton Suhadolc and Suhadolc's memories of Plečnik.

B. Podrecca, R. Teichräber, D. Prelovšek. "Jože Plečnik, architetto sloveno." *Casa Vogue* 170 (January 1986).

Publications from Establishments where Plečnik Taught

Styl 4 (1913), pp. 176–192.

Iz ljubljanske šole za arhitekturo. Ljubljana, 1923. Selection of architectural works.

Iz ljubljanske šole za arhitekturo. Ljubljana, 1925. Selection of architectural works.

J. Plečnik: Výběr prací školy pro dekorativní architekturu v Praze z roku 1911–1921. Prague, 1927. Selection of works by students at the Prague School of Architecture.

J. Plečnik. *Lučine. Iz ljubljanske šole za arhitecturo 1928.* Prague, 1928. Teachings at the Ljubljana School of Architecture.

Lučine. Nadaljevanje. 118 izbranih del arhitekov Tehnike Univerze ljubljanske 1929–1937. Ljubljana, 1937. Photo album of projects entitled "Works of Architects from the Superior Technical School of Ljubljana."

Zbornik oddelka za arhitekturo na Univerzi v Ljubljani 1946–1947. Ljubljana, 1948. Newsletter from the Architecture Department at the University of Ljubljana, including projects by Plečnik and his students.

Illustration Credits

F. Burkhardt Archives: 70, 89, 90 (bottom), 91 (top), 110 (right), 134 (top and bottom right), 140 (bottom), 142, 143.

Director of Museums for the City of Vienna: 19.

D. Gale: 139, 168 (except top left), 169 (except top right), 170 (except top left, top center), 171 (except top and bottom right), 172 (except top right, bottom left, bottom right), 174 (except top left, center, center right), 175 (top center, bottom left).

N. Gattin and N. Vranić: 121 (bottom), 122 (top), 124 (top), 125 (top right), 130 (bottom), 141, 145 (top), 149 (bottom), 158.

L. Gostiša: 91 (bottom), 131 (bottom).

J. Kališnik: frontispiece.

Matkovič Collection: 51.

Ljubljana Museum of Architecture: 4–12, 27–44, 53–57, 58 (top), 62 (top right, bottom), 67–69, 72, 73, 76 (top), 77 (bottom), 81 (right), 90 (top), 99, 102 (left), 110 (left), 125 (top left, bottom), 126–128, 130 (top), 131 (top), 132, 133, 134 (top left), 135–138, 148 (bottom).

M. Nikolič: 188–196.

F. Pace: 117 (bottom).

B. Podrecca Archives: 120 (top), 140 (top), 145 (bottom).

D. Prelovšek: 159 (top).

E. Primozič: 75, 76, 77 (top), 79, 81 (left), 114, 115 (left), 116, 117 (top), 129, 144, 146, 147, 148 (top), 149 (top), 150–152, 153 (bottom, drawing by J. Valentinčič), 154, 155, 157, 159 (bottom), 160–165.

K. Řepa: 119.

V. Slapeta Archives: 57 (top), 58 (bottom), 59, 60, 62 (top left), 63, 83, 86, 93, 99 (right), 115 (right), 169 (top right).

K. Tahara: 123 (bottom).

Zacherl Collection: 123 (top).